THE BOOK OF PATRIOTIC HOLIDAYS

The Book of
PATRIOTIC
HOLIDAYS

Marguerite Ickis

With drawings by Miriam F. Fabbri

DODD, MEAD & COMPANY   NEW YORK

TO MY FATHER

American patriot for ninety-eight years

CONTENTS

THE BOOK OF PATRIOTIC HOLIDAYS

1. HOW TO USE THIS BOOK

The text in this book may be regarded as a patriotic reader—full of pertinent fact as to the history of our country and the men who made it; or, it can be considered as a "how to do it" book, with all kinds of ideas that can be used in patriotic programs. While the subject matter is built around the nation's holidays, many other facts are included because they are involved to some extent with these holidays.

With the richness of material to choose from, the decision of what to use was the greatest problem. Three of our patriotic holidays celebrate the memory of great American heroes—Abraham Lincoln, George Washington and Christopher Columbus. We decided to develop these chapters along the lines of human interest stories and incidents of pageantry, rather than writing of the subjects' philosophies and heroism. We felt this type of material would be excellent for use in dramatics, story hours or festivals.

While this book has no formal patriotic programs, it has enough games, dances, songs, etc., for many, many celebrations. All the material is written on a patriotic theme and much of it is interchangable from one chapter to another. We believe it is more fun if the participants select activities that are suitable for their own age groups and surroundings. Any city or town wishing to plan a community program for a patriotic holiday should be able to find just the material they need, be it a play day, a pageant, a festival or . . . a shindig!

If the songs, games and dances in this book seem old-fashioned, it is because we selected only ones that fit the different periods in American history. All the material in this book (with the exception, perhaps, of the stories by the Reverend Weems) is authentic

1

as far as we know. Today we are so surrounded by the influences of technology and mass production that we are apt to forget that our main root was planted by our forefathers many years ago; and from it stems our rich national heritage. It is very important to remind our children that this is so.

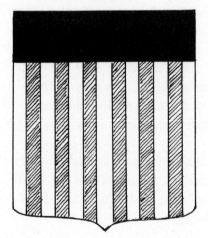

2. SYMBOLS OF THE UNITED STATES

Coat of Arms of the United States

The coat of arms of the United States is shown on the opposite page.

Eagle. The eagle is the American, or bald eagle.

Shield. On the eagle's breast is the *shield of the United States*, consisting of thirteen vertical stripes, typifying the thirteen original states. The shield, or escutcheon, is borne on the breast of the American eagle without any other "supporter," denoting that the United States of America relies on its own virtue—in other words, the nation stands on its own feet for right and justice.

Chief. The blue "chief" (upper part of shield), which from a heraldic standpoint unites the whole, represents Congress. "E *pluribus unum*" ("One out of many") always alludes to this union, whose strength and preservation depend upon Congress.

Olive branch and arrows. The olive branch and arrows (thirteen) in the talons of the eagle denote the power of peace and war which is exclusively invested in Congress.

Crest. The crest over the head of the eagle shows thirteen stars breaking through a cloud, denoting a new constellation in the firmament of sovereign powers.

Colors. According to the records of the Department of State, the following is the significance of the colors in the shield: *red* signifies hardness and valor; *white* symbolizes purity and innocence; *blue* represents vigilance, perseverance and justice.

Use. The coat of arms of the United States should be used only by those who are authorized to do so by law or custom. Under no circumstances should either the coat of arms or the shield of the United States be used for advertising or other commercial purposes.

3

It should be noted that the number of red and white stripes in the shield of the United States and in the flag are reversed—that is, in the flag there are seven red and six white stripes, while in the shield there are six red and seven white stripes.

The American Eagle and Other Symbols

Before the Revolution, the American Indian served as a symbol of the new continent. But after independence had been won and a permanent government established, emblems of a patriotic nature, like the flag and the American eagle, were adopted as national symbols. This was most important—we think unconsciously in symbols, and they became symbolic of America's dreams.

The American eagle became the patriotic emblem after it had been adopted by Congress in 1782 for the great seal of the United States. Emblematic eagles had been used in the colonies before this time, but the American bald-headed species were specifically designated as the eagle of the great seal. Bald means white, because the eagle has a white head and tail feathers.

The Stars and Stripes and eagles were not the only symbols used for patriotic expression—there were words as well:

Freedom acquired a particular importance because of the Declaration of Independence. It was a symbol of America's greatest dream.

Liberty. The profile of her head appeared on various American coins and was made into statues, weathervanes, inn signs, etc.

Columbia. A symbol used in much the same way as "Liberty." She is often depicted as a counterpart to Uncle Sam.

Justice. A figure with bandaged eyes holding the balanced scales. It was often seen on early courthouses.

The eagle shown on page 5 is in an attitude of defiance, prepared to stand its ground. This is an interpretation of a new country, sensitive and proud of its new strength. The eagle was a favorite motif used by craftsmen in colonial days as a decoration. Among examples in museums today are stenciled eagles on furni-

SIMPLIFIED EAGLE DESIGN USED AS A WALL DECORATION. THE STENCIL WAS CUT BY AN ITINERANT DECORATOR IN WASHINGTON, CONN. (1772-79).

ture, carved wooden eagles, ships' heads, metal door knockers and weathervanes, and designs of quilts and coverlets.

Homage to the Flag by an Eagle

While they were hoisting the Stars and Stripes over the officers' headquarters of Camp Curtain, near Harrisburg, Pennsylvania, in the spring of 1861, and just as the men had seized the halyards, a large eagle that came from no one knows where hovered above the flag, and sailed majestically over the encampment while the flag was run up.

Thousands of eyes were upturned in a moment, and as the noble bird looked down, the cheers of three thousand men rent the air! Never was such an ovation paid the "imperial bird of Jove." It lingered for a few moments, apparently not a particle frightened at the terrific noise, then cleaving the air with its pinions, disappeared in the horizon.

3. HOW TO MAKE A PATRIOTIC MURAL

A mural, according to Webster's dictionary, is a painting on a wall. In this broad definition, almost any large picture can be termed a mural, so let us discuss some various types:

Cyclorama. This was the project of William Wehner from Milwaukee, Wisconsin. His best-known work, or cyclorama, is the great "Battle of Atlanta," which depicts the entire battlefield. He imported twelve experienced artists from Germany who had been working on glorifying the Germans in the Franco-Prussian wars. Three of the artists worked on landscapes, five painted figures, and the rest painted animals. The artists worked from a high platform in the middle of the battlefield from which they could view the entire area. The finished paintings were mounted in a room with circular walls, thus showing the entire field from the artist's point of view.

FIGURE 1

Frieze. The correct use of a frieze is in architecture—it is used to connect arches, pillars or columns. It runs horizontally and is usually decorated in figures, sculptured in relief. However, a more liberal definition would be: Any ornamented band on a wall with repeated motifs or representing a story. The story of Columbus would make an excellent theme. Cut long strips of paper 12 to 14 inches wide and paint in the main episodes in his life *in chronological order.* You can make cutouts from colored construction paper if you prefer to use them for characters.

7

FIGURE 2

Collage means an agglomeration of fragments pasted together. It is a method employed by twentieth-century artists in introducing paper or nonpigmented materials in a painting. This technique is becoming more and more popular in schools and among hobbyists and decorators who want to add a design or color to a room. If you wish to make a patriotic collage, cut a piece of Masonite or heavy cardboard the size you want and paint in a background. It can be plain, or you may add figures. Now add objects cut from cloth, paper, metal—anything you like. The subjects can be a liberty bell, military buttons, insignia, eagle, etc. It is best to keep the design abstract, paying attention to placing the elements in proper balance and adding rhythm to the composition. If you were making a marine collage, you would paint the sea as a background and then add real shells, bits of seaweed, sand, starfish, etc.

Mural. The type of murals we are going to talk about is the kind that can be used in a schoolroom and executed by a number of children. Each must have a theme, a story and characters. To illustrate how to develop such a project, we are going to select the theme "Abraham Lincoln" and relate it in Chapter 4 of this book. However, you will soon see that these techniques can be applied to any of the other patriotic holidays.

Begin a mural by cutting a strip of wrapping paper the length and width you desire. It can be made to fit one end of a wall in a classroom, or if the school has a long hall or corridor, each grade may contribute a panel of different stories on the same theme. Select the characters you are going to use and draw them any size as they will undoubtedly be reduced or enlarged on the final mural in order to fit them to scale.

	1	2	3	4	5	6	7	8	9	10
A	A 1	A 2	A 3	A 4						
B	B 1	B 2	B 3	B 4						
C	C 1	C 2	C 3	C 4						
D	D 1	D 2	D 3	D 4						

FIGURE 3. CARICATURE OF MURAL

The next step is to make a caricature of the mural like the one in Figure 3. It need not be the actual size of the mural—the squares are used for placing characters and deciding on their colors. Later, they can be made to scale by reproducing outlines and curves in the same relative position in a larger or smaller square.

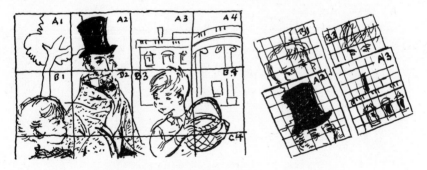

FIGURE 4. HOW TO ENLARGE A DESIGN

If you are to work on only one segment of the mural, your assignment might be "Squares A2, A3, B2, B3, C3, C4." By checking the caricature, you can locate your squares—but more than likely you will be handed the original squares to duplicate. If these squares are large, fill them with little squares and make your own caricature. Try to reproduce the characters in the exact relative positions in which they must fit later with the whole.

9

FIGURE 5. CENTRAL FIGURE

The easiest method to use in assembling characters is to have a large background figure that depicts the theme. It not only serves as a focal point, but ties the picture together. We have chosen to paint the White House, as most of the stories have to do with Lincoln while he was President. If the incidents were mostly about his childhood, we might have drawn a log cabin or, for Memorial Day, the Lincoln Memorial. The characters should be grouped carefully to complete a pleasing design and the colors properly distributed.

FIGURE 6. A PANORAMA

A *Panorama* can be defined as a scene passing continuously before the vision. If you want to make this type of mural, place the characters in small groups, according to the story, and then in a continuous line. In this case, an artist should add some scenery such as buildings or trees to tie the theme together—this will also add different heights to the picture. Green is an excellent color for blending in the brighter, more dominant ones.

"Constitution and the Union—Harmony and Prosperity to all."—LINCOLN.

PRESIDENT,
ABRAHAM LINCOLN.
VICE-PRESIDENT,
HANNIBAL HAMLIN.

4. ABRAHAM LINCOLN'S BIRTHDAY — FEBRUARY 12

If one were to ask which patriot in American history is most loved and honored, the answer very likely would be "Abraham Lincoln." Perhaps it is because, to quote Carl Sandburg, he represents humanity. It is difficult, indeed, to select material out of all that has been written about the life of Lincoln and apply it to a birthday celebration. We decided to devote the chapter to stories and incidents about him that will appeal to young and old alike. They can be dramatized, used as a theme for murals, or just read.

We hope some of the stories will be new to you. They are taken from books written shortly after Lincoln's death by people closely associated with him and the White House, such as Ward Hill Lamon and William H. Herndon, Lincoln's law partners. The stories about Tad Lincoln and the President's two goats were told by Elizabeth Keckley. She was a former slave who became modiste to Mrs. Lincoln and, after the President's death, her best friend. It was due to her efforts that Mrs. Lincoln was able to sell her clothes and jewelry to pay her debts and also to raise sums of money that maintained a home for her and the children.

11

As Told by a Neighbor

Abe loved to lie under a shade tree or up in the loft of the cabin and read, cypher, and scribble. At night he sat by the chimney "jamb" and cyphered by the light of the fire, on the wooden fire shovel. When the shovel was fairly covered, he would shave it off with his father's drawing knife and begin again. In the daytime he used boards for the same purpose, out of doors, and went through the shaving process everlastingly. If there was a passage he didn't understand, he would write it down on boards until he could get some paper. Then he would rewrite it, look at it, repeat it.

Books that he read were *Aesop's Fables*, *Robinson Crusoe*, Bunyan's *Pilgrim's Progress*, a *History of the United States*, and Weems' *Life of Washington*.

One day, Lincoln borrowed Weems' *Life of Washington* from his neighbor, Josiah Crawford. He read it with great avidity and, when not in use, carefully deposited it on a shelf made of clapboard. But unfortunately there was a big crack between the logs in the wall behind it; and one night, while Abe was dreaming in the loft, a storm came up, and the rain, blown through the opening, soaked his precious book from cover to cover. Crawford was a sour, churlish fellow at best, and flatly refused to take the damaged book back again. He said that if Abe had no money to pay for it, he could work for it. He was obliged to pull fodder for three days, at twenty-five cents a day.

For a long time there was only one person in the neighborhood for whom Abe felt a decided dislike; and that was Josiah Crawford, who made him pull fodder to pay for the Weems' *Washington*. Just the same he had to have work, and was often hired by his old adversary at twenty-five cents a day. Besides, the family was in possession of several books he wanted to read and one of them was the *Kentucky Prospector* from which he learned his school orations.

The time came when Lincoln got his revenge for all this petty brutality. Crawford was as ugly as he was surly. His nose was a monstrosity, long and crooked, with a huge misshapen "stub" at the end. The whole was as "blue" as Mr. Crawford's spirits. Upon this member Abe leveled his attack in rhyme, song and chronicle; and though he could not reduce the nose, he gave it fame from the Wabash to the Ohio! His sallies upon this single topic achieved him a great reputation as a "poet" and a wit and caused Crawford intolerable anguish.

In school Abe was a good student and speller. When he was fifteen his teacher, Andrew Crawford, proceeded to give a lesson in good manners once a week. One scholar was required to retire and reeenter as a polite gentleman is supposed to in a drawing room. He was received at the door by another scholar, and conducted from bench to bench until he had been introduced to all "young ladies and gentlemen" in the room.

Crawford by no means neglected to teach the children to spell. One day he gave out the difficult word "defied" and the whole class failed to spell it. "Defide" said one; "d-e-f-y-d-e," said another; "DEFYED, DEFYED," cried another, and another. Crawford's wrath gathered and he said he would keep them after school. Among them was a Miss Roby, a girl of fifteen, who saw Lincoln at the window—he had his finger in his eye, and a smile on his face. She took the hint to change the letter "y" to "i" and the class was let out.

How Lincoln Won His First Dollar

When Lincoln was about eighteen years of age, he constructed a little flat boat, large enough to take a barrel or two of things plus a few bundles down the river to New Orleans. There were no wharves in those days and it was customary, if there were passengers at any of the landings, for them to go out in a boat and the steamer would stop and pick them up. Two men came down to the shore in a carriage, with trunks, and after looking over all the boats, asked "Who owns this one?" and Abe replied "I do." "Will you," said one of them, "take us and our trunks out to the steamer?" "Certainly," said Abe. They got on board and he lifted up their heavy trunks and put them on deck of the steamer. Each of them took from his pocket a silver half dollar and threw it down on the floor of the boat. Years later Lincoln said:

"Gentlemen, you may think it a very little thing, and in these days it seems to me like a trifle, but it was a most important incident in my life. I could scarcely credit that I, a poor boy, had earned a dollar in less than a day—that by honest work I had earned a dollar. The world seemed wider and fairer before me. I was a more hopeful and confident being from that time."

While his boat was loading at Gentry's Landing, Lincoln saw a great deal of the pretty Miss Roby. One evening, said she, "Abe and I were sitting on the banks of the Ohio and I said that 'the sun was going down.' He said to me 'That's not so; it don't really go down, it seems so. The earth turns from west to east, and the revolution of the earth carries us under as it were; we do the sinking, as you call it.' I replied, 'Abe, you are a fool!' but now I know he was right."

On a winter's morning Lincoln might be seen stalking toward the market house, basket on arm, his old gray shawl wrapped around his neck, and his little boy, Willie or Tad, asking a thousand questions. He frequently went to his neighbor's house for milk. Their rooms were low and he said one day, "Jim, you'll have to lift your loft a little higher—I can't straighten up." He then turned to the wife who was short of stature and remarked that "little people had some advantages; they required less wood and wool to make them comfortable."

From Lincoln's Scrapbook

> Time! What an empty vapor 'tis!
> And days how swift they are;
> Swift as an Indian arrow,
> Fly on like a shooting star.
> The present moment just is here,
> Then slides away in haste,
> That we may never say they're ours,
> But only say they are past.

A group from a Philadelphia political organization called at the White House to pay their respects to Lincoln. The chairman of the body in presenting one of the members said:

"Mr. President, this is A. B. Sloanaker, a most active and earnest friend of yours. He has, among other things, been good enough to paint and present to our league rooms a most beautiful portrait of yourself."

Lincoln took Mr. Sloanaker's hand in his, and with an earnest cordiality shook it kindly, saying:

"I presume, sir, in painting your beautiful portrait, you took your idea of me from my *principles* and *not* from my person."

Lincoln's Public Days

It was President Lincoln's custom to hold one or two "public days" a week when he received all applicants in their turn. One time, Major Hay saw Mr. Lincoln escorting an elderly lady out to the door and, as she lingered, heard him say:

"I am really very sorry madam; very sorry. But your own good sense must tell you that I am not here to collect small debts. You must appeal to the courts in regular order."

When she left, Mr. Lincoln sat down, crossed his legs, locked his hands over his knees and remarked:

"What odd people come in to see me and what odd ideas they must have about my office! I feel—though the tax on my time is heavy—that no hours of my day are better employed than those that bring me again within direct contact and atmosphere of the average of our whole people. Many of the matters brought to me are utterly frivolous but all serve to renew in me a clearer and more vivid image of that great popular assemblage out of which I sprang, and to which at the end of two years I must return. . . . I tell you, Major, that I call these receptions my *public opinion baths*, for I have little time to read the papers and gather public opinion that way; and though they may not be pleasant in all particulars, the effect, as a whole, is renovating, and invigorating to my perception of responsibility and duty."

A committee of clergymen called one day upon Lincoln and the spokesman poured forth a lecture which was fault-finding from beginning to end. It was delivered with much energy, and the shortcomings of the administration were rehearsed with painful directness. Lincoln's reply was a notable one—he said:

"Gentlemen, suppose all the property you possess were in gold and you had placed it in the hand of Blondin to carry across the Niagara on a rope. With slow, cautious steps he walks the rope, bearing your all, would you shake the cable, and keep shouting to him, 'Blondin! stoop a little; go a little faster; lean more to the south! now lean a little more to the north!'—would that be your behavior in such an emergency? No; you would hold your breath, every one of you, as well as your tongues. You would keep your hands off until he was safe on the other side. This government, gentlemen, is carrying an immense weight; untold treasures are in its hands. The persons managing the ship of state in this storm are doing the best they can. Don't worry them with needless warnings and complaints. Good day, gentlemen. I have other duties pressing upon me I must attend to."

Three stories told by Elizabeth Keckley

Mr. Lincoln was fond of pets. He had two goats that knew his voice and when he called them, they would come bounding to his side. On warm bright days he and Tad would sometimes play in the yard with these goats, for an hour at a time.

One bright day, the President walked to a window and, looking down, said:

"Madame Elizabeth, come here and look down at my two

goats. I believe they are the kindest and best goats in the world. See how they sniff the clear air, and skip and play in the sunshine. Whew! What a jump!" he exclaimed, as one of the goats made a lofty spring. Musing a moment, he continued: "He feeds on my bounty, and jumps with joy. Do you think we should call him a *bounty jumper?* But I flatter the bounty jumper. My goat is far above him. I would rather wear his horns and hairy coat through life, than demean myself to the level of the man who plunders the national treasury in the name of patriotism. The man who enlists in the service for a consideration, and deserts the moment he receives his money but to repeat the play, is bad enough; but the man who manipulates the grand machine and who simply makes the bounty jumper his agent in an outrageous fraud is much worse."

Only a moment the shadow rested on his face. Just then both goats looked up at the window and shook their heads, as if to say "How d'ye, old friend?" "See," exclaimed the President, "my pets recognize me. How earnestly they look!"

The only article of furniture, so far as I know, that was taken away from the White House by Mrs. Lincoln was a little dressing stand used by the President. I recall hearing him say one day:

"Mother, this little dressing stand is so handy, and suits me so well, that I do not know how I shall get along without it when we move away from here." He was standing before a mirror brushing his hair when he made the remark.

18

"Well, Father." said Mrs. Lincoln, "if you like the stand so well, we will take it with us when we go away."

"Not for the world!" he exclaimed, but she interrupted him;

"I should like to know what difference it makes if we put a better one in its place."

"That alters the question. If you will put a stand in its place worth twice as much as this one, and the Commissioner consents, then I have no objection."

Mrs. Lincoln remembered these words, and with the consent of the Commissioner took the stand to Chicago for the benefit of little Tad. Another stand, I must not forget to add, was put in its place.

After his father's death, Mrs. Lincoln was determined that Tad should have a lesson every day, and he was given a book by his mother. She seated herself in an easy chair and Tad sat in a low chair by her side. He opened his book and began to spell slowly the first word, "ape."

"Well, what does a-p-e spell?"

"Monkey" was the instant rejoinder.

The word was illustrated by a small woodcut of an ape, which looked to Tad's eyes very much like a monkey, and his pronunciation was guided by the picture and not by the sounds of the different letters.

"Nonsense!" exclaimed his mother. "A-p-e does not spell monkey."

"Does spell monkey! Isn't that a monkey?"

"No, it is not a monkey."

"Not a monkey—what is it?"

"An ape."

"An ape! 'Taint an ape. Don't I know a monkey when I see it?"

"No, if you say that is a monkey."

"I do know a monkey. I have seen lots of them in the street with the organs. I know a monkey better than you do; 'cause I always go out into the street to see them when they come by, and you don't."

"But, Tad, listen to me. An ape is a species of monkey. It looks like a monkey, but is not a monkey."

"It shouldn't look like a monkey then. . . ."

It was his brother Robert who finally succeeded in convincing Tad that a-p-e does not spell monkey.

"Lincoln never read any other way than out loud," so said his law partner. Lincoln's explanation was: "When I read aloud two senses catch the idea; first, I see what I read; second, I hear it, and, therefore, I can remember better."

Lincoln's Dream
(as told to Ward Hill Lamon)

"It seems strange how much there is in the Bible about dreams. There are, I think some sixteen chapters in the Old Testament and four or five in the New in which dreams are mentioned; and there are many other passages scattered throughout the book which refer to visions. If we believe the Bible, we must accept the fact that in the old days God and His angels came to men in their sleep and made themselves known in dreams. Nowadays dreams are regarded as very foolish, and are seldom told except by old women and young men and maidens in love.

"About ten days ago," said he, "I retired very late. I had been up waiting for important dispatches from the front. I could not have been long in bed when I fell into a slumber, for I was weary. I soon began to dream. There seemed to be a deathlike stillness about me. Then I heard subdued sobs, as if a number of people were weeping. I thought I left my bed and wandered downstairs. There the silence was broken by the same pitiful sobbing, but the mourners were invisible. I went from room to room; no living person was in sight, but the same mournful sounds of distress met me as I passed along. It was light in all the rooms; every object was familiar to me; but where were all the people who were grieving as if their hearts would break? I was puzzled and alarmed. What could be the meaning of all this? Determined to find the cause of a state of things so mysterious and shocking, I kept on until I arrived at the East Room, which I entered. There I met with a sickening surprise. Before was a catafalque, on which rested a corpse wrapped in funeral vestments. Around it were stationed soldiers who were acting as guards; and there was a throng of people, some gazing mournfully upon the corpse, whose face was covered, others weeping pitifully. 'Who is dead in the White House?' I demanded of one of the soldiers. 'The President,' was his answer; 'he was killed by an assassin!' Then came a loud burst of grief from the crowd, which awoke me from my dream. I slept no more that night. I have been strangely annoyed by it ever since."

21

Abraham Lincoln

by William Cullen Bryant

O, slow to smite and swift to spare!
  Gentle and merciful and just!
Who in the fear of God didst bear
  The sword of power—a nation's trust.

In sorrow by thy bier we stand
  Amid the awe that hushes all,
And speak the anguish of a land
  That shook with horror at the fall.

Thy task is done—the bonds are free;
  We bear thee to thy honored grave,
Whose proudest moments shall be
  The broken fetters of the slave.

Pure was thy life; its bloody close
  Has placed thee with the sons of light,
Among the noble hosts of those
  Who perished in the cause of right.

Sermon

by Henry Ward Beecher

Four years ago, O Illinois, we took from your midst an untried man, and from among the people. We return him to you a mighty conqueror. Not thine any more but the nation's; not ours, but the world's. Give him place, O ye prairies! In the midst of the great continent his dust shall rest, a sacred treasure to myriads who shall pilgrim to that shrine to kindle anew their zeal and patriotism. Ye winds that move over the mighty places of the West, chant his requiem! Ye people, behold a martyr whose blood, as so many articulate words, pleads for fidelity, for law, for liberty.

5. GEORGE WASHINGTON'S BIRTHDAY—
FEBRUARY 22

A number of states claim the honor of holding the first Washington's Birthday celebration; but one thing is sure, it soon became a national holiday for everyone. One of the first official celebrations was held in New Port, Rhode Island, in 1781, and the next year in Virginia there was another, just before Washington became President. The most touching claim is one made by New Jersey, based upon an incident "when the artillery bands played before Washington's tent on a wintry February 22nd at Valley Forge." When Washington was fifty, a great banquet was held in New York attended by eminent dignitaries and statesmen, and it was then decided to make his birthday a yearly celebration. Special songs and poems have been written for the occasion, among them one by the poet Will Carleton:

> February—February—
> How your moods of action vary
>   Or to seek or shun;
> Now a smile of sunlight lifting
> Now in chilly snowflake drifting;
> Now with icy shuttles creeping
>   Silvery webs are spun.
> Now, with laden torrents leaping
>   Oceanwards you run.
> Now with bells you blithely sing

23

'Neath the stars or sun;
Now a blade of burdock bring
   To the suff'ring one;
February you are very
   Dear, when all is done;
Many blessings rest above you
You, who one day (and so we love you)
Gave us Washington.

George Washington had many facets to his personality—stern-ness as a soldier, dignity as a statesman, and strength as father of his country. Other facets were the virtues and exploits bestowed upon him by the Reverend Mason Locke Weems in stories that have caused much controversy and furor among historians and matter-of-fact people.

We decided to read the *History of George Washington* by Rev-erend Weems and found the stories not only delightful, but beautifully written. Would not a Washington Birthday party be dreary indeed without the usual cherries and hatchets for decora-tion? And who among us can truthfully deny a story that was told so many years ago by "An excellent Old Lady," "A distant relative," or "an Old Gentleman who attended the same school with George"? Anyway, we are presenting Reverend Weems' case as he stated it along with several stories in the original text:

"Of private deeds of Washington very little has been said—In most of the elegant orations pronounced to his praise, you see nothing of Washington below the clouds. Oh no! Give us his private virtues that lay the foundation of all human excellence. To them his private character is everything; his public hardly anything. Give us his private virtues! In these every youth may become a Washington, a Washington in piety and patriotism—in industry and honor—and consequently a Washington in what alone deserves the name, Self Esteem and Universal Respect.

"Who among us can hope that his son shall ever be called, like Washington, to direct the storms of war, or to ravish the ears of deeply listening Senators? To be constantly placing him before our children, in this high character, that is like springing in the clouds a Golden Pheonix which no mortal calibre can ever hope to reach. Or like setting pictures of the Manna before the mice, who 'not all the manna of Heaven' can ever raise to equality."

A Peep Show

Children might like to use the following stories about George Washington as subjects for a peep show. This type of show was very popular in colonial times, both for children and adults. The adult shows were usually in taverns. They cost a penny a look, and the scenes were usually such that they could not be shown in the open. About the only peep shows used today are for decoration inside Easter eggs.

DETAILS OF PEEP SHOW

To make a peep show select a box, remove the lid and fit a mirror on the wall of one end. In the opposite end cut a small hole for the "peeping." Cut out trees, shrubs, flowers, etc., and landscape the bottom of the box (old Christmas cards are an excellent source). Now place in any characters you like—George cutting down the cherry tree for instance—and avoid placing tall or large objects in the center that would be in a direct line with the peep hole. Cover the top of the box with a sheet of tracing paper which will give indirect lighting to the scene. The mirror at the end will give an illusion of space.

TYPES OF PEEP SHOWS

FOUR STORIES BY PARSON WEEMS

The Virtue of "Sharing"
(as related to Mr. Weems by an aged lady—a distant relative)

One fine morning [in the fall of 1737], Mr. Washington having little George by the hand, came to the door and asked my Cousin Washington and myself to walk with him to the orchard promising he would show us a fine sight. On arriving at the orchard, we were presented with a fine sight indeed! The whole earth as far as we could see was strewn with fruit; and yet the trees were bending under the weight of the apples, which hung in clusters like grapes, and vainly strove to hide their blushing cheeks behind the green leaves. Now, George, said his father, look here, my son! don't you remember when this good cousin of yours brought you that fine large apple last year, how hardly I could prevail on you to divide with your brothers and sisters; though I promised you that if you would but do it, God Almighty would

26

give you plenty of apples this fall. Poor George could not say a word; but hanging down his head looked quite confused, while with his little naked toes he scratched in the soft ground. . . .

George looked in silence on the wild wilderness of fruit. He marked the busy humming bees, and heard the gay notes of the birds; then lifting his eyes, filled with shining moisture, to his father, he softly said, "Well, Pa, only forgive me for this time; and see if I ever be so stingy any more."

The Virtue of "Truth"

Never did the wise Ulysses take more pains with his beloved Telemachus, than did Mr. Washington with George to inspire him with an early love of truth. "Truth, George," said he, "is the loveliest quality of youth. I would ride fifty miles, my son, to see the little boy whose heart is so honest, and his lips so pure, that we may always depend on every word he says—But, Oh George, how different is the case with the boy who is so given to lying that nobody can believe a word he says! He is looked at with aversion wherever he goes. It would be hard for me to give you up, whose little feet are always so willing to run about with me, but still I would give you up rather than see you a common liar."

"Pa," said George very seriously, "do I ever tell lies?"

"No, George, I thank God you do not, my son; and I rejoice in the hope you never will."

The following anecdote is a case in point—it is too valuable and too true to be doubted; for it was communicated to me by the same excellent lady to whom I am indebted for the last—

"When George," said she, "was about six years old, he was made the wealthy master of a hatchet! of which, like most little boys, he was immoderately fond and was constantly going about and chopping everything that came in his way. One day, in the garden, where he often amused himself hacking his mother's peasticks, he unluckily tried the edge of his hatchet on the body of a beautiful young English cherry tree, which he barked so terribly, that I don't believe the tree ever got the better of it. The next morning the old gentleman, finding out what had befallen his tree, which, by the by, was a great favorite, came into the house; and with much warmth asked for the mischievous author, declaring at the same time, that he would not have taken five guineas for his tree—"George," said his father, "do you know who killed that beautiful little cherry tree, yonder in the garden?" This was a tough question; and George staggered under it for a moment; but he quickly recovered himself and looking up at his father, with the sweet face of youth brightened with the inexpressible charm of all-conquering truth, he bravely cried out, "I can't tell a lie, Pa, you know I cant' tell a lie; I did cut it with my hatchet." "Run to my arms, my dearest boy; glad am I, George, that you killed my tree; for you have paid me for it a thousand folds. Such an act of heroism in my son is more worth than a thousand trees, though blossomed with silver, and their fruits of purest gold."

Virtue—Belief in God

Mr. Washington conducted his son with great ease and pleasure along the paths of virtue. To startle George into a lively sense of his Maker, he fell upon the following very curious and impressive expedient:

One day he went into the garden and prepared a little bed of finely pulverized earth, on which he wrote George's name in full, in large letters—then strewing in plenty of cabbage seeds, he covered them up and smoothed all over nicely with a roller. This

bed he purposely prepared along with ripe fruit, he knew would be honored with George's presence every day. Not many mornings had passed away before in came George, his eyes wild rolling, and his little cheeks ready to burst with great news:

"O Pa! come here! come here!"

"What's the matter, my son, what's the matter?"

"O come here, I tell you Pa; come here! and I will show you a sight as you never saw in all your life" and he pointed to the large letters in all the freshness of the newly spring plants, the full name

GEORGE WASHINGTON

"But Pa, who did make it there? who did make it there?"

"It grew there by chance, I suppose, my son."

"Oh Pa, you must not say chance did all of this and I daresay now Pa, you did it just to scare me."

"Well, George, you have guessed right, I indeed did it; but not to scare you, my son, but to learn you a great thing which I wish you to understand. I want, my son, to introduce you to your true Father."

"But, Pa, where is God Almighty! I never did see him yet?"

"True, my son, but though you never saw him, yet he is always with you. You did not see me when ten days ago I made this little plant bed, where your name is in such beautiful letters, yet you know I was here!

"Well then, and as my son could not believe that chance had made and put together his name (though only sixteen letters), then how can he believe that chance could make and put together those millions and millions of things that are exactly fitten to his good! . . .

"When he looks down into the water he sees beautiful silvery fishes for him! and up in the trees there are the apples, the peaches and thousands of sweet fruit for him! and all, all around him, wherever my dear boy looks, he sees everything just to his wants and wishes—the bubbling spring, with cool, sweet water for him to drink! the wood to make him sparkling fires when he is cold! and beautiful horses for him to ride! and strong oxen to work for him! and the good cow to give him milk! and the bees to make sweet honey for his sweeter mouth! the little lambs with snowy wool for beautiful clothes for him! Now these and all the ten thousand other good things, more than my son can ever think of, and all so exactly fitten to his use and delight— Now how could chance ever have done all this for my little son. Oh George!"

He would have gone on, but George had had enough.

"Oh, Pa, it can't be chance that made and gave me all these things."

"What was it then, do you think, my son?"

"Indeed, Pa, I don't know unless it was God Almighty!"

"Yes, George, it was, my son, and nobody else!"

Colonel Lewis, Washington's playmate and kinsman, has been heard to say that he has often seen him throw a stone across the Rappahannock, at the lower ferry of Fredericksburg. It would be no easy matter to find a man nowadays who could do it.

Tableau Vivant

Here is an interesting way to show a tableau—we might call it one that has an introduction. A narrator stands on one side of the stage as shown in the illustration and the tableau is formed on the other inside a large frame. The frame is covered with a thin material, such as theatrical gauze or fish net, during the main introduction, allowing the audience to see a misty picture of the group. At the end of the narrative, the curtain is removed and the characters are in full view.

In this type of tableau the introduction is important. Try to find some interesting angle to tell—it might have to do with history, background, relate it to other events, etc. Make the curtain raising be a climax of something, either with a spotlight on the frame or vivid colored costumes.

On the following pages in this book you will find episodes in the life of Washington that have color and pageantry suitable for this type of production. We have chosen a minuet that was danced before Martha Washington. The introduction can tell something of the history of the dance, how it was danced on state occasions, etc.

Pas Grave

Slow, grave step—Stand in fifth position (right foot in front) and bend both knees, count 1;

Rise on both toes, count 2;

Drop weight on left heel, count 3;

Repeat, stepping forward with right foot, etc., count 4-5-6.

Pas Marche

March step—A simple, smooth walking step, a step to each beat in the measure. In walking, the front part of the foot should touch the floor first and the heel last.

Pas Balance

Balance step—This step may be used as a balance forward or backward, and is sometimes used as a progressive movement.

To balance forward: Step forward upon right foot, count 1; and extend toe of left foot to left side, weight still on right foot, count 2-3.

To balance backward: Step back on left foot and extend toe of right foot to right side, count 4-5-6.

If used as a progressive movement: Step forward on right foot, count 1;

Slide toe of left foot to left side, count 2;

Draw left foot to right, count 3 (weight is on right foot during all 3 counts);

Step forward on left foot, count 4;

Toe of right foot to side, count 5;

Draw right to left, count 6 (weight is on left foot during last 3 counts).

Pas Minuet

Minuet step—Start from fifth position (right foot in front); bend both knees, rise, and glide the toes of the right foot to the right side, count 1;

32

Transfer weight to right foot and extend left foot to side, heel raised, count 2;

Bend right knee and draw left foot, with slightly bent left knee, to back of right, count 3;

Rise to full height on both toes, stretching both limbs, and transfer weight to left foot, count 4 (right foot is in fifth position);

Glide right foot to right side, count 5;

Draw left foot back of right, left knee bent, count 6.

To move to left side: Start with left foot in fifth position front.

Pas Boure

Place right foot back of left (both knees slightly bent) and then step to left side with left foot. Repeat with right foot back as long as desired. If moving to the right, place left foot back of right.

Pirouette

Turning step—Step to right side with right foot, bring left foot in front and around to the rear of the right foot, and in this position turn on both toes.

Assemble

Bring the feet together, either in first or fifth position.

Pas Sissone

Slide the toe of the right foot back of left foot and bend both knees, count 1;

Slide ball of the left foot to the left side, count 2;

Slide right foot forward in fifth position, count 3;

Continue as long as desired. To move to the right, reverse the movements.

MINUET DANCED BEFORE MARTHA WASHINGTON

Washington the President

After the Revolution, Washington had only one desire and that was to turn the government over to the people. This was one instance in history when a successful military leader had a deep and earnest desire to send back his soldiers to civilian life without using his forces for any personal ambitions of his own (as Napoleon did, for instance). When he put the civil government into peaceable possession of Congress, it meant constituting a representative government for his country without a trace of military leadership. What is more, he left a trained army to back up the peace. In his speech before Congress he said:

"There is a respect due to the United States among nations which will be withheld, if not absolutely lost, by a reputation of weakness; if we desire to avoid insult we must be able to repel it, if we desire to secure peace."

Washington was the unanimous choice of the people for first President of the new nation. This was in the year 1789 and the following is a description of the first inauguration as told by R. M. Devens in his book *Our First Century*:

"Upon leaving Alexandria, Washington was accompanied by great throngs of people all the way to New York which was then the nation's capital. At Philadelphia, he was received by a concourse of the most distinguished personages of the city and state, followed by thousands of people to a grand banquet. The next day, at Trenton, he was welcomed in a manner exceedingly novel and touching. On the bridge extending across the stream which passes through the town, a triumphal arch was erected with

evergreens and floral adornment and supported by thirteen pillars similarly wreathed.

"On the front was inscribed in large gold letters "the Defender of the Mothers will be the Protector of the Daughters." Over this, in the center of the arch, was a dome or cupola of evergreens and flowers and the words "To You Alone." The ladies wore white dresses and six of these held baskets of flowers in their hands, and they strewed flowers before the General.

"At Brunswick, he was joined by the Governor of New Jersey and other dignitaries who were to accompany him to New York. They embarked on a magnificently decorated barge, managed and rowed by thirteen pilots, attired in white. Arriving at New York, Washington was met by the governor of the state, immense crowds, and there were many other barges filled with eminent dignitaries from all parts of the land. He found multitudes of his old faithful officers and men around him to offer their congratulations. But when a group of soldiers appeared to escort him to the Capital he said:

" 'I require no guard but the affection of my people.'

"On Thursday, April 3, 1789, the ceremony of inaugurating the first President of the United States took place in New York. The Hudson was studded with boats bearing visitors and long caravans of carts began to arrive. Every tavern and boarding house was filled and many persons slept in tents. At eight o'clock on this memorable morning the sky was overcast and the appearance was that of a gathering storm. However, the moment the bells started to ring, the sky cleared and the weather was serene and beautiful.

"The ceremony of the day was ushered in by a salute fired from the battery at six o'clock in the morning. At nine, church bells rang out a merry peal, at ten they summoned the worshipers to church, each pastor devoting the occasion to imploring Heaven's blessings upon the nation and the first President.

"General Washington proceeded to Federal Hall where the Senate was assembled. At the door, he was met by the vice-president who said:

" 'Sir, the senate and house of representatives of the United States are ready to attend you to take the oath required by the Constitution, which will be administered to you by the chancellor of New York.'

" 'I am ready to proceed,' was Washington's reply, made with his accustomed elegant dignity."

It is said that Washington, on taking oath, laid his hand upon the page in the Bible containing the fiftieth chapter of Genesis. That memorable volume now belongs to one of the Masonic lodges in New York.

Washington believed, with good reason, that prestige was important in world affairs. The United States was young and shaky, and he wanted to give it dignity comparable to the courts of Europe. The President's coach was a canary yellow decorated with guilt cupids and nymphs. It was drawn by six white horses—

the grooms not only brushed their teeth, but each night rubbed white marble paste on their hoofs and let it dry to a shiny gloss. The following is an eyewitness account of the President's arrival in Philadelphia for his second inauguration:

"The crowd gradually opened and gave space for the approach of an elegant white coach, drawn by six superb white horses, having in its four sides beautiful designs of the four seasons, painted by Capriani. It slowly made its way until it drew up immediately in front of the Hall.

"But as the coach door opened, there issued from it two gentlemen, with long white wands, who, with some difficulty, parted the people, so as to open a passage from the carriage to the steps. As the person of the President emerged from the carriage, a universal shout rent the air, and continued as he deliberately mounted the steps.

"Never did a more majestic personage present himself to the public gaze. He was dressed in a full suit of the richest black velvet; his lower limbs in short clothes with diamond knee buckles, and black silk stockings. His shoes, which were brightly japanned, were surmounted with large silver buckles. His hair, carefully displayed in the manner of the day, was richly powdered, and gathered behind in a black silk bag, on which was a bow of black ribbon. In his hand he carried a plain cocked hat, decorated with the American cockade. He wore by his side a light slender dress-sword, in a green shagreen scabbard, with a richly ornamented hilt."

George Washington served his country well as President for eight years. He refused the third term, a rule that held for the next 144 years. After retiring to his beloved home, Mount Vernon, he did not live long to enjoy it, as he died at the age of sixty-seven. Thomas Jefferson wrote of him later:

"He was indeed a wise man, a good and a great man. His integrity was most pure; his justice the most inflexible I have ever known. He was incapable of fear, meeting personal dangers with the calmest unconcern."

REVOLUTIONARY WAR UNIFORMS

In Memoriam

Never has the memory of any American patriot been more honored than that of George Washington, who was "first in war, first in peace, and first in the heart of his countrymen." Streets, cities and states throughout the nation bear his name, his statues stand in public squares of many cities—even in far away Budapest. Perhaps the most familiar memorial is the Washington Monument in the nation's capital, which reaches 555 feet up into the sky and overlooks the Potomac River. The work was begun in 1828 and completed in 1884.

The cornerstone was laid July 4, 1848. The honoring procession was the most splendid ever seen in Washington. Included in the march were the most important personages, Congress, the military; and, as the bells chimed solemnly, it took them a full hour to reach the Monument. Most interesting were the Indians—Cherokee, Chickasaw, Choctaw, Creek and Sawbridge—all tribes Washington had dealt with during his lifetime. They brought with them silver metals, struck in 1786, representing Washington shaking hands with the red man. These they placed reverently in the cornerstone. Among numerous other articles distributed there were placed two daguerreotypes, one each of Martha and George Washington. The ceremony ended with the stirring words of Daniel Webster:

"Let it rise! let it rise! till it shall meet the sun in his coming! let the earliest light of the earliest morning gild it, and the parting day linger and play on its summits."

WASHINGTON BICENTENNIAL

This great celebration of the two hundredth anniversary of Washington's birth took place all over the United States during 1932. It opened New Year's Eve by the striking of a clock belonging to Washington's mother, Mary Ball Washington, and it was heard from coast to coast by radio. The formal celebration lasted from February 21 until Thanksgiving and programs usually included speeches, parades and waving of flags. In Washington, the

WASHINGTON BICENTENNIAL ISSUE

celebration was opened by President Hoover and the singing of "America" by 12,000 persons.

Stamp with Polish Heroes

The Polish representative was present to receive a special commemorative stamp issued for the occasion. It depicted George Washington in the center with Polish heroes of the Revolution on either side, namely, Pulaski and Kosciusko. The United States Post Office also issued a special series of twelve stamps, each showing Washington as he was painted or sculptured by a famous artist. (See page 41.)

"In All, Himself"

Washington, the brave, the wise, the good,
Supreme in war, in council, and in peace,
Valiant without ambition, discreet without fear,
Confident without presumption,
In disaster, calm; in success, moderate; in all,
    himself;
The hero, the patriot, the Christian,
The father of nations, the friend of mankind,
Who, when he had won all, renounced all,
And sought in the bosom of his family and of
    nature, retirement,
And in the hope of religion, immortality.
           —Inscription on Washington's Tomb
           (Author unknown)

6. PAN AMERICAN DAY—APRIL 14

> "God has made us neighbors;
> let justice make us friends."
> —WILLIAM JENNINGS BRYAN

Each year Pan-American Day and Week are designated by official proclamation throughout the Western Hemisphere as an occasion on which Americans of all ages and nationalities unite in a spirit of friendliness and understanding. It is still a very young holiday, and since the languages spoken in most of the South American countries are Spanish or Portuguese, program material is hard to come by. President Hoover asked that the day be observed in all schools with appropriate ceremonies and that flags be flown from all public buildings. When President Kennedy took office he was specific in his desire to bring about a close relationship with our southern neighbors when he said: "The need is urgent. The task is staggering. There is no time to be lost."

The need for an united America was first conceived by Simón Bolívar in 1815. He was the military liberator of South America and is considered the greatest hero in the Southern Hemisphere. In his "Jamaica Letter" he wrote:

"More than anyone, I desire to see America fashioned into the

43

greatest nation in the world; greatest not so much by virtue of her area and wealth, as by her freedom and glory."

The first American conference was held in Panama in 1826, when governments of Spanish colonies of South America and Central America were represented at a meeting. The United States sent no representative and it was not until 1889 that another effort was made to organize the Western Hemisphere countries. The Conference lasted six months in Washington, D.C., and James G. Blaine, Secretary of States, was elected chairman and a charter was formed. In 1910 the name "Pan-American Union" was adopted and in 1930, Congress set aside April 14 as a national holiday. The date was chosen because the Union was officially designated on April 14, 1889.

In 1901, there was a Pan-American Exposition in Buffalo, New York, to demonstrate our new consciousness of our southern neighbors and show a spirit of international loyalty. The "theme" of the Exposition was "to show progress made in industries, arts, and sciences by American republics during the Nineteenth Century." People came from all over the world to see the "Rainbow City," so named because of the beautiful lights and colors. We might recall the sad note injected into the celebration when President McKinley was assassinated.

The Pan-American Building was built in 1910 largely through the efforts of Andrew Carnegie. This building is truly the "House of the Americas," its ownership shared by all the citizens of the twenty-one member nations of the Organization of American States:

We are all—

AMERICANS

Argentine, Bolivia, Brazil, Chile, Colombia, Costa Rica, Cuba, Dominican Republic, Ecuador, El Salvador, Guatemala, Haiti, Honduras, Mexico, Nicaragua, Panama, Paraguay, Peru, United States, Uruguay and Venezuela.

The Pan-American Building

This distinctive white marble building, situated in the midst of beautifully landscaped gardens, has a patio, balconies, tiled roof and decorative details typical of Latin America. Here one finds Maya, Toltec, Aztec, Inca and other Indian designs, as well as examples of Spanish colonial architecture.

Concerts are held in the Aztec Garden behind the building when the weather is suitable. A blue-tiled lily pool, guarded by the figure of Xochipilli, the Aztec god of flowers, is the central feature of this formal garden. On the arched terrace are blue tiles inlaid with Maya figures of carved wood.

The tunnel under Eighteenth Street, connecting the main building with the Administration Building, is unique because of the 480-foot mural painted on the entire length of one of its side walls. Called the world's longest mural, its brilliant panels represent "Roots of Peace." On the opposite wall appear quotations from the speeches and writings of great patriots and statesmen.

On the patio are exotic plants typical of a tropical garden. The large fountain, illuminated at night, has figures on its shaft representing an Aztec warrior, a woman symbolizing the future and the early American as the European explorers found him. The center basin is decorated with eight feathered serpents and figures representing three types of Indian art—Aztec, Mayan and Zapotecan. The patio floor is of a mosaic design copied from Maya and Inca ruins. On the walls above are the shields of the various member countries (and Canada), alternating with plaques bear-

45

ing the names of men who led the movement for independence in their respective countries.

On the second floor is the art gallery, with exhibits of works from all the American republics. Another room is called the "Hall of Heroes": it displays the flags of the twenty-one countries. Busts of national patriots stand on marble pedestals.

The Hall of Americas is used for international conferences and meetings, concerts, lectures, Pan-American Day celebrations and diplomatic banquets. It has crystal chandeliers by Tiffany and stained-glass windows portraying the arms of the republics and other details. The busts of Andrew Carnegie and Leo S. Rowe, Director General of the Pan-American Union for twenty-six years, stand on either side of the stage.

Program Material

One of the services of the Pan-American Union is to unite the peoples of the twenty-one American republics. Americans as widely separated as those of Alaska and Punta Arenas, Chile, come to know each other better through special observances, classroom projects, club programs, plays and pageants, parades and social events. The Pan-American Union is ready to give out facts about our neighbors, and for this purpose they have a large assortment of printed program material ready for mailing. You can write for their *Short List of Publications* (in English and Spanish) about the twenty-one American republics. The booklets range in price from 10¢ to 50¢ and here are a few subjects:

Folk Songs and Stories of the Americas.
Christmas in Latin America.
Folk Songs and Dances No. 1.
Folk Songs and Dances No. 2.
Some Latin-American Festivals and Folk Dances.
Music of Latin America.

Another excellent source for any type of a recreation program is the Cooperative Recreation Service, Delaware, Ohio. They have been publishing small booklets (approximately thirty-two pages) over a period of twenty-five years that may be purchased in larger volumes under the trade name of "Handy." They have two booklets of Latin-American folk music and games—*Raque Ran* and *Amigos Cantando*. The text of the songs is written both in the native language and in English translation.

The Cooperative Recreation Service kindly gave us permission to use songs and games from these booklets and we have selected the following:

Lament - *Huainito*

Trans. by Olcutt Sanders   Argentine Folk Song

Slowly

Two lit-tle doves were sit-ting to-geth-er, cry-ing so;
Who could it be who's tak-en your soft wings, lit-tle dove?
Dos pa-lo-mi-tas se la-men-ta-ban llo-ran-do;
¿Quién te ha con-ta-do tus be-llas o-las, pa-lo-ma?

One to the oth-er in con-so-la-tion mur-mured low:
Who is the false one who took ad-van-tage of your love?
Y la u-na a la o-tra se con-so-la-ban di-cien-do:
¿Q al-gún fal-sa-rio ha sor-pren-di-do tu-vue-lo?

CHORUS

Ah, ah, ah,   lit-tle dove, Who is the
Ah, ah, ah,   pa-lo-ma, ¿Q al-gún fal-

false one who took ad-van-tage of your love?___
sa-rio ha sor-pren-di-do tu vue-lo?___

2. It was a villain to whom I gave my wings one day
   He needed wings so we could together fly away.
   Sweet were his words, so I gave my wings
       that he might fly
   When he'd deceived me, he left me helpless
       here to die
   Cho. Ah, ah, ah, sweet his words,

47

When he'd deceived me, he left me
helpless here to die.

2. Quiso el ingrato que yo mis alas le diera,
Para ir volando los dos juntitos al cielo.
Por su cariño le dí mis alas y luego,
Abandonada de desengaño me muero.
Cho Ah, ah, ah, y luego
Abandonada de desengaño me muero.

The "*Huainito*" is a general name for a song form.

Ten Puppies,—*Los Diez Perritos*

Trans. by Olcutt and Phyllis Sanders   Puerto Rican Folk Song

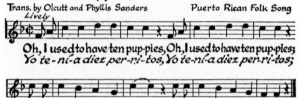

Oh, I used to have ten pup-pies, Oh, I used to have ten pup-pies;
Yo te - ní-a diez per-ri-tos, Yo te-ní-a diez per-ri-tos;

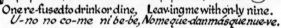

One re-fused to drink or dine, Leav-ing me with on-ly nine.
U-no no co-me ni be-be, No me que-dan más que nue-ve.

2. |: Oh, I used to have nine puppies,:|
One choked on a cake I baked,
Leaving me with only eight.
3. |:...eight...:| One a blade sent off to heaven,....seven.
4. |:...seven...:| One with water would not mix,...six.
5. |:...six...:| One not looking took a dive,...five.
6. |:...five...:| One liked footlight glamor more,...four.
7. |:...four...:| One turned wrongside out, you see,....three.
8. |:...three...:| One caught cold from heavy dew,....two.
9. |:...two...:| One was taken with a gun,....one.
10. This one went just as he came,
Leaving me with but his name.
And his name I don't recall.
Of my song this must be all.

Mr. Snail, Snail, Snail,–Caracol-col-col

Moderato
Montevideo, Uruguay

Mis-ter snail, snail, snail, sun your horns and do not fail,
Ca-ra-col-col-col, sa-ca tus cuer-nos por el sol.

For it's kill'd you'll sure-ly be when they come down from the sea.
Ya vie-nen de ma-tar por la o-ri-lla del-mar.

Latin-American Carnival

One can usually find a small procession winding through the streets of a South American city every hour of the day. These processions are usually religious in character, but many of them take place during carnivals, traditional holidays or fiestas. The indoor celebrations are comparatively few, as the weather in most of the southern countries is so mild that people spend most of their time in their patios or courtyards, and meet on the public square for public events.

In offering the following suggestions, no attempt has been made to give a definite plan for a carnival. In fact, the main events, such as vendors, strolling entertainers, dances, etc., can

49

be applied to any theme for a patriotic program. A Latin-American carnival would be an excellent "special day" event for camps to stimulate interest in the customs and music of the Good Neighbor children.

In South America the majority of people wear clothes similar to those worn in the United States and Europe. Only natives in the interior, or Indians, wear the gaily colored costumes. The Pan-American Union feels that it is very important to stress this fact, particularly since many geographies give children the impression that South America is peopled by uncivilized tribes. In keeping with this request, it is suggested that costumes be limited to the vendors and entertainers.

Strolling Entertainers should be dressed in native costume. They represent the South American natives who come to the city on market days. They may stroll in groups or singly, according to the instruments they play. We suggest that all during the carnival a number of small processions take place at different intervals during the day. This would be more in keeping with local customs than one big parade to open the celebration. The processions may be enlivened by the antics of:

The Happy Man, who takes the place of the proverbial clown so amusing to our own American children. He wears a large straw hat with a gaily colored costume; or

A Man on Stilts—also dressed in bright colors.

One Man Orchestra. This musician carries several kinds of native instruments tied around his neck. The number depends upon his versatility in playing them. He plays them in turn to suit his fancy or to please the crowd.

A Special Opening. A carnival should have a focal point and a

formal opening of some kind. Plan some interesting exhibits for the people to examine while the crowd is gathering. They may be Latin-American stamps, travel posters from various countries or educational posters telling about industrial products, architecture, foods, etc. See if you can discover some Pan-American crafts decorated in original designs and find information as to their origin.

New York City, in 1960, saluted Pan-American Week with seven days of speeches, parades, song and dance festivals, etc. The opening ceremony was one that could be used by any city or town regardless of size. Attractive girls in their picturesque and colorful costumes blended the soil of  their native countries into a caldron as a symbol of inter-American friendship. Mayor Wagner later turned the first spade full of this blended earth in the planting of the "Good Neighbor Tree" in City Hall Park. A Fire Department color guard carried the massed colors of the twenty-one American republics.

Decorations. In planning decorations for a Pan-American affair, one constantly thinks of bright colors such as red, yellow, green, orange and blue. Even the flowers associated with these countries are brilliant in hue—the geranium, hibiscus, dahlia. The zinnia is a native flower of Mexico. Colors found in these different flowers are reflected in the people's dress and crafts. You may add atmosphere to the streets and grounds by hanging strings of colored gourds and dried peppers, baskets of melons, etc. Of course, you will get your best color effects by using flags of the twenty-one American republics.

Children with Flower Hoops. The decoration on a hoop can be adapted to the occasion. For little parades or fiestas flowers are most colorful. Sometimes streams of ribbon or paper are tied to the rims so they can wave in the breeze, or small ornaments and bright packages are put there for color. Flowers can also be tied to jumping ropes for exhibition games or dances.

The Kite is a popular toy all over Central and South America, even more popular than in the United States, and is called "El Cometa" (the comet). The shape is usually a hexagon, the sticks are bamboo, and the covering tissue paper. When a boy wants to show his artistic taste he ornaments his kite with a fringe of tissue paper around the bottom; and if he is musical he extends the sticks above the paper at the top and stretches across them strips of hides, which in a strong breeze give a beautiful sound like an aeolian harp. A musical chord can be made by loosening or tightening the strings.

The Morral or grab-bag is a common and popular game. Sometimes it is filled with gifts, comical or otherwise, concealed in packages, that are drawn by people present. Or again mottoes are placed in a bag to be taken out by the players and read for the amusement of the company.

A popular game played both indoors and out is "The Prop and the Money." A ring is drawn upon the floor or upon the ground, about a yard in diameter, and a section of a bamboo, twelve to eighteen inches long, is set up in the center, with a penny on top. The players stand off a certain distance, and with pennies or nuts endeavor to knock the coin from the top of the stick. If it falls within the ring the player loses or forfeits the penny. If it falls outside the ring it is his.

It would be in keeping with the South American custom to serve food at the carnival that can be cooked out-of-doors. Charcoal burners are found on the streets, particularly near the market places. They are used for cooking anything from tamales to coconut candy. Here is a tortilla vendor's song:

The Tortilla Vender
El Tortillero

Trans. by Olcutt Sanders   Chilean Folk Song

Thru the dark-ness now I wan-der With a lan-tern for my
No-che o-scu-ra, na-da ve-o Pe-ro lle-vo mi fa-

light.__ Past your door-way I am go-ing; So I'll
rol;__ Por tus puer-tas voy pa-san-do, y can-

REFRAIN
sing a fond good-night.__ Now__with deep sad-ness__
tan-do con a - mor.__ Mas,__ voy can-tan-do__

My__wares I cry them.__Who'll buy my good__ to - sta-
con__ har-ta pe - na.__ ¿Quien com-pra mis__ to-sta-

1. i - tas?__ Tor - ti-llas! Buy them! 2. Buy them!
i - tas?__ Tor - ti-llas bue-nas? bue-nas?

2. Oh, my fair one, why so heartless?
    To my song you don't reply
    As I wander past your doorway
    And sing out my vendor's cry.
3. Well, goodbye, then. I am leaving
    With my basket and my lamp,
    Since you will not give an answer,
    Just as if I were a tramp.

Here are some amusing ways to serve food at an open-air carnival:

FRUIT IN A CART   FROM A STICK   FROM A CHARCOAL BURNER

Vendors. In South America, the vendors usually live many miles from the cities and bring their native crafts and fruits to sell on market days. Usually very poor and having no money to pay for booths or stalls at the market, they display their wares on the ground, or walk about the streets carrying them in different ways. One quaint custom prevailing in many of the old Mexican markets is the displaying of fruits, melons or vegetables in groups of threes. They are always placed to form a triangle with two on the bottom and one on the top. Peanuts are even displayed in this fashion! The triangle is sacred to many of the Indian tribes and is reflected in designs woven into blankets or painted on pottery. The vendors shown on page 55 are typical of ones found on South American streets.

Musical Instruments

The guitar is the universal musical instrument in South America. It does not always have six strings; it is known as a trace if it has three strings and a quatro if it has four strings. The accordion is used in Argentina and Peru. The violin is also found in the South American cities.

Congas. These are large drums made by fastening stays of wood together with hoops of metal or wood. They are larger around at the top than at the bottom and stand on the ground while being played. They are about 3½ feet in height.

Maracas are instruments made from gourds of various shapes. To make one rattle, cut a hole in the top and bottom of a gourd, and use a stick for a handle. Before the handle is inserted, put some rice or dried beans inside the gourd.

Castanets. The delight of all with their clicks and rattling thrill, they enhance the dance beyond measure and can be played by the smallest child. Expensive to buy, they can be made from a scrap of any fine hardwood. If the castanets are to be used by children, fasten them to a central piece of wood to which is attached a handle about six inches long.

TYPES OF VENDORS

Latin-American Dances

The tango, rumba and conga are among the favorite ballroom dances in this country and it should not be difficult to find the music and someone to teach the steps in any community. One dance you will surely want to include at a carnival is:

The Conga. This is danced to the rhythm of conga drums and other percussion instruments. It was originally danced at night or in the jungles, and the drums were placed on the ground so the natives could dance around them to the rapid beat of the drums. Their leader carried a flaming torch or a lantern high in the air and everyone swayed back and forth with the light. Since the original dance resembles our game "Follow the Leader," a conga dance would be an excellent climax to a carnival.

Mexican Hat Dance. This is danced by a boy and a girl. During the first part of the dance, the boy makes advances to the girl to the quick tempo of any South American music. She is shy until he takes off his large sombrero and throws it on the ground in front of her. . . . If she loves him, she dances inside the rim of the hat; if not, she dances around it.

Broom Dance. The man in the illustration with mops and brooms is in reality a peddler trying to sell his wares. Once in a while he will do a dance to draw attention of the crowd or to relieve the monotony of a dull day of trading. This may be used as a comedy number in a dance program.

A part of the material used in this chapter is taken from a small booklet, *A Pan-American Carnival,* published by the National Recreation Association, 8 West Eighth Street, New York 11, N.Y. The music is from the Cooperative Recreation Association, Delaware, Ohio.

My Twenty Pennies

Trans. by J. Olcutt Sanders   Venezuelan Folk Song

1. With twen-ty pen - nies, with twen-ty pen - nies, with twen-ty
1. Con real y me - dio, con real y me - dio, con real y

pen - nies I bought a pa - va. The pa - va had a pa-
me - dio Compre una pa - va. La pa - va tuvo un pa-

vi - to. I have the pa - va and the pa-vi - to;
vi - to. Ten-go la pa - va, tengo el pa-vi - to y

And thus I have yet   My twen - ty pen - nies.
siempre me que - do   mi   real y me - dio.

2. Gata, (cat); gatico, (kitten)   5. Lora, (parrot); lorito.
3. Chiva, (goat); chivito.   6. Vaca, (cow); vaquito.
4. Mona, (monkey); monito.   1 (Pava, - turkey.)
*Repeat in each stanza after the first, with all previous animals.

With This Half Dollar - Con Este Medio

Trans. by Olcutt and Phyllis Sanders   Puerto Rican Folk Song

Quickly

With this half dol-lar I car-ry for spend-ing, With this half
Con es-te me-dio que trai-go, que ven-do, Con es-te

dol-lar I car-ry for spend-ing,   I buy the ca-sa,
me-dio que trai-go, que ven-do, Com-pro la ca-sa,

and the ca-se-ro; And then I have yet all my di-ne-ro.
com-pro el ca-se-ro; Siem-pre me que-da el mis-mo di-ne-ro.

2. Tinta, (ink); tintero, (inkwell).
3. Finco, (farm); finquero, (farmer).
4. Silla, (chair); sillero, (chairmaker).
5. Leche, (milk); lechero, (milkman).
6. Cabra, (goat); cabrero, (goatherd).

Casa, - house; casero, - householder; dinero, - money.
*These two measures, repeated in each stanza with all the
previous purchases, are sung as fast as possible.

The Little Boat
El Barco Chiquitito

Trans. by Olcutt Sanders   Latin-American Folk Song

There was a lit, a lit, a lit-tle boat out
Es-te_e-ra_un bar, un bar, un bar-co chi-qui-

in the sea; There was a lit, a lit, a lit-tle
ti - to. Es-te_e-ra_un bar, un bar, un bar-co

boat out in the sea; There was a lit, a lit, a
chi-qui-ti - to; Es-te_e-ra_un bar, un bar, un

lit-tle boat out in the sea, That just could not be, That
bar-co chi-qui-ti - to, Que no po-dí-a, Que

just could not be, That just could not be made to sail.
no po-dí-a, Que no po-dí-a na-ve-gar.

2. So passed one, two, three, four, five, six,
   seven weeks or more, (3)
   And its provisions (3) all did fail.

3. If this simple story is too short to please you, (3)
   We can again tell (3) this same tale.

*2. Pasaron una, dos, tres, cuatro, cinco, seis,
   semanas,(3)
   Y los víveres (2) empezaron a escasear.*

*3. Y si la historia os parece corta,(3)
   Volveremos (3) a empezar.*

This is a Spanish version of a song better known in French.

Fray Martín

Trans. by Olcutt and Phyllis Sanders   Latin-American Round

Fray Mar-tin goes up the tow-er, Then be-gins to
Fray Mar-tín al cam-pa-na-rio, Su-be y to-ca

ring the hour:— Tan! Tan! Tan! Tan!
la cam-pa-na: ¡Tan! ¡Tan! ¡Tan! ¡Tan!

Fray Martín, (Fry Mar-teen') means Friar Martín.

This is the Latin-American counterpart of LOVELY EVENING.

7. MEMORIAL DAY—MAY 30

Our Memorial Day custom of decorating graves stems from ancient festivals, both in Europe and Asia. In China and Japan the celebration is known as the Feast of Lanterns, and in Italy people go to the churchyards on All Souls Day to lay garlands of flowers on the graves. It is interesting to note that France also observes May 30 as a legal holiday to commemorate the day when Napoleon's ashes were brought to Paris from St. Helena. They call it the "Day of Ashes."

The custom of decorating the graves of our dead with flowers stems from a paragraph printed in the New York *Tribune* two years after the Civil War ended. It stated: "The women of Columbus, Mississippi, have shown themselves impartial in their offerings made to the memory of the dead. They strewed flowers alike on the graves of the Confederate and of the National soldiers." The North was thrilled with this show of tenderness, and the incident became a symbol of bringing about amity and understanding between the states. It was this occasion that inspired Francis Miles Finch to write his moving lyric, "The Blue and the Gray":

> By the flow of the inland river
> Whence the fleets of iron have fled,
> Where the blades of the grave grass quiver,
> Asleep are the ranks of the dead:
> Under the sod and the dew,
> Waiting the judgment-day;
> Under the one, the Blue,
> Under the other, the Gray.

59

So with an equal splendor,
The morning sun-ray fall
With a touch impartially tender
On the blossoms blooming for all;
Under the sod and the dew
Waiting the judgment-day;
Broidered with gold, the Blue,
Mellowed with gold, the Gray.

So, when the summer calleth,
Our forest and field of grain,
With an equal murmur falleth
The cooling drip of rain.
Under the sod and the dew,
Waiting the judgment-day;
Under the rain, the Blue,
Wet with the rain, the Gray.

Sadly, but not with upbraiding,
The generous deed was done;
In the storm of the years that are fading,
No braver battle was won;
Under the sod and the dew,
Waiting the judgment-day;
Under the blossoms, the Blue,
Under the garlands, the Gray.

No more shall the war cry sever,
Or the winding rivers be red;
They banish our anger forever
When they laurel the graves of our dead!
Under the sod and the dew,
Waiting the judgment-day;
Love and tears for the Blue,
Tears and love for the Gray.

On Memorial Day the flag is displayed at half-staff from sunrise until noon and at full staff from noon until sunset. (This does not apply to flags on sidewalks.)

Memorial Day is not a religious festival but a patriotic observance. In the past, it has been regarded as a "symbol" in the North to dissolve old differences and to honor the memory of brave men who died in the defense of their country. The parades are no longer headed by the tottering feet of veterans of the Grand Old Army; much of the significance of the day has passed with them. The following facts are recorded for the benefit of a generation which may consider the Grand Army as a mere handful of old soldiers who have all ceased to be:

Grand Army of the Republic

The Grand Army of the Republic held their first "Encampment" at Indianapolis, November 20, 1866. The purpose was to secure funds to help soldiers who were lying in hospitals and to rehabilitate bereft families of veterans. More generous pension laws and other legislation of advantages for their members was brought about by the influence of important members of the G.A.R.

It is a remarkable fact that all but one of our seven Presidents elected immediately following the Civil War were eligible for the G.A.R. (Grant, Hayes, Garfield, Arthur, Harrison and McKinley): still more remarkable that one state, Ohio, should have furnished five of these six—plus two other notable military leaders, Sherman and Sheridan.

But membership was not confined to the illustrious. All ranks and grades were laid aside under the mantle of the order and its basic principles of fraternity, charity and loyalty. There was no discrimination as to creed, party, color, birthplace or social standing.

The inevitable decline of the G.A.R., owing to a constantly increasing death rate, began in the mid-nineties and continued to spread as time took its toll of advancing age. In the year 1902 alone more than 50,000 members passed away. In May, 1949, an exhaustive survey published by *Life* magazine showed thirty members were still living, their ages ranging from 100 to 110. But some three months later *The New York Times* reported that this remnant of the original army had diminished to a mere sixteen surviving veterans, only six of whom were able to attend the eighty-third and final "Encampment" on August 31, 1949. Of these six—the oldest of whom was James A. Hard, 108, of Rochester, New York—all were afficted with deafness, four were confined to wheel chairs and one was blind. The blind delegate was "Uncle Joe" Clovese, the nation's last Negro Civil War veteran, who was born in slavery and deserted his master to take part in the siege of Vicksburg with the Union armies. Mr. Clovese died in Detroit, Michigan, on July 13, 1951, at the age of 107.

At this memorable meeting in Indianapolis the last executive leader, 100-year-old Commander-in-Chief Theodore A. Penland of Portland, Oregon, feebly sounded "Taps" with a short but solemn requiem: "I close this final meeting of the Grand Army of the Republic." Their flags, medals and other relics are now in the Smithsonian Institution in Washington. Books, records and other official papers can be found in the Library of Congress.

In 1917, the annual reunion of the Confederate Veterans was held in Washington. For the first time, the veterans marched side by side with brothers in blue down Pennsylvania Avenue and were reviewed by the President.

On July 2, 1938, President Roosevelt dedicated a monument on Oak Hill in Gettysburg called the "Eternal Light Peace Memorial." A Union soldier of the G.A.R. and a Confederate soldier

62

from Georgia unveiled it. The shaft rises fifty feet above the ground and can be seen for twenty miles. The inscription on the monument reads: "An enduring light to guide us in unity and fellowship."

Washington's Prayer

Every day at noon a litany and prayers are said for the nation in the Washington Memorial Chapel at Valley Forge. Upon the altar of this chapel is placed an illuminated copy of Washington's prayer for the nation:

"Almighty God, we make our earnest prayer that Thou wilt keep the United States in Thy holy protection; that Thou wilt incline the hearts of all the citizens to cultivate a spirit of subordination and obedience to the government; and entertain a brotherly affection and love for one another and for their fellow citizens of the United States at large.

"And finally that Thou wilt most graciously be pleased to dispose of all of us to do justice, to love mercy, and demean ourselves with that charity, humility, and pacific temper of mind which were the characteristics of the Divine Author of our blessed religion and without a humble imitation of whose example in these things we can never hope to be a happy nation.

"Grant our supplication, we beseech Thee, through Jesus Christ our Lord, Amen."

A beautiful custom observed on Memorial Day in important ports in the United States is to set afloat tiny boats filled with flowers in memory of those who have died at sea. The Navy also follows this custom in honor of their brave heroes who went down at sea in defense of their country.

The Flag in Church

Since many patriotic speeches and orations are given on Memorial Day it is good to know how the United States flag should be displayed in a church:

If in the chancel—The flag is in the position of honor at the

clergyman's right as he faces the audience, and the church or other flag is at his left. (See drawing.)

If outside the chancel—The flag is in the position of honor at the right of the congregation as it faces the clergyman, and the state or other flags are at its left.

MEMORIAL DAY ORATIONS

From General Sheridan

For four long bitter years the mighty tide of war rolled through the land, engulfing in its crimson flood the best and bravest of the North and South, bearing their souls outward with resistless sweep, to the dread sea whose shores to human eyes are viewless, whose somber waves are ever chanting solemn requiems for the dead! In this wild storm of war the banners of the South went down. The bells of liberty through all the land rang out a joyous peal of welcome, and the guns from fortress, field, and citadel thundered greeting to the hour that proclaimed America one and indivisible. From Southern gulf to Northern lakes, from Northern lakes to Atlantic and Pacific coasts, we were ONE. The Mississippi flowed not along the border of a dozen empires; the blue waters of the lakes beat not upon the shores of rival governments; the mountains of the land frowned not upon hostile territories; the ocean bore not upon its bosom the fleets of contending states; but over all the land a single flag flew out its folds, symbol of victory, index of a reunited people.

Our Country's Defenders

by William McKinley

Blessed is that country whose soldiers fight for it and are willing to give the best they have, the best that any man has, their own lives to preserve it because they love it. Such an army the United States has always commanded in every crisis of her history. From the war of the revolution to the late Civil War, the men followed the flag in battle because they loved that flag and believed in what it represented.

This was the stuff of which the volunteer army of '61 was made. Every one of them not only fought but thought. And many of them did their own thinking and did not always agree with their commander. A young soldier in the late war was in the battle line ahead with the color guard, bearing the stars and stripes way in front of the line, but the enemy still in front of him. The general called out to the color-bearer "Bring those colors back to the line," and, quicker than any bullet that young soldier answered back, "Bring the line up to the colors!" It was the voice of command; there was a man behind it, and there was patriotism in his heart.

> So nigh is grandeur to our dust;
> So near is God to man,
> When duty whispers low, "Thou must,"
> The youth replies, "I can."

And so more than two million brave men thus responded and made up an army grander than any army that ever shook the earth with its tread, and engaged in a holier cause than ever engaged soldiers before.

What defenders, my countrymen, have we now? We have the

65

remnant of this old magnificent, matchless army, of which I have been speaking, and then as allies in any future war, we have the brave men who fought against us on the Southern battlefields. The army of Grant and the army of Lee are together. They are one now in faith, in hope, in fraternity, in purpose, and in an invincible patriotism. And therefore, the country is in no danger. In justice strong, in peace secure, and in devotion to the flag all one.

Address Delivered Memorial Day, 1884, at Keene, New Hampshire

by Oliver Wendell Holmes, Sr.

I think that, as life is action and passion, it is required of a man that he should share the passion and action of his time at peril of being judged not to have lived. . . .

Accidents may call up the events of war. You see a battery of guns go by at a trot, and for a moment you are back at White Oaks swamp, or Antietam, or on the Jerusalem Road. You hear a few shots fired at a distance, and for an instant your heart stops as you say to yourself, The skirmishers are at it, and listen for the long roll of fire from the main line. You meet an old comrade after many years, he recalls the moment when you were nearly surrounded by the enemy, and again there comes up to you that swift and cunning thinking on which hung life or freedom— shall I stand the best chance if I try the pistol or the saber on that man who means to stop me? Will he get his carbine free before I reach him, or can I kill him first? These and a thousand other events we have known are called up, I say, by accident, and apart from accident, may be forgotten.

But as surely as this day comes around, we are in the presence of the dead. For one hour at least, on this day when we decorate our graves, the dead come back and live with us. I see them now, more than I can number, as once I saw them on the earth. They are the same bright figures, or their counterparts, that come also before your eyes; and when I speak of those who were my brothers, the same words describe yours.

CIVIL WAR UNIFORMS

Strike for that broad and goodly land
  Blow after blow; till men shall see
That *might* and *right* move hand in hand,
  And glorious must their triumph be!

He sleeps where he fell, 'mid the battle roar,
  With his comrades true and brave;
And his noble form we shall see no more—
  It rests in a hero's grave.

Address

by Henry Ward Beecher

Oh, tell me not that they are dead—that generous host, that airy army of invisible heroes! They hover as a crowd of witnesses above this nation. Are they dead that yet speak louder than we speak, and a more universal language? Are they dead that yet act? Are they dead that yet move upon society, and inspire the people with nobler motives and more heroic patriotism?

Every mountain and hill shall have its treasured name, every river shall keep some solemn title, every valley and every lake shall cherish its honest register; and till the mountains are worn out, and the rivers forget to flow—till the clouds are weary of replenishing springs, and the springs forget to gush, and the rills to sing, shall their names be kept fresh with reverent honors which are inscribed upon the book of national remembrance!

Who Goes There

by Thomas Curtis Clark

Who goes there, in the night,
  Across the storm-swept plain?
We are the ghosts of a valliant war—
  A million murdered men!

Who goes there, at the dawn,
  Across the sun-swept plain?
We are the hosts of those who swear;
  It shall not be again!

8. FLAG DAY—JUNE 14

THE FLAG

Due to lack of records kept during the anxious months of the Revolution, there are many theories of the "true" beginning of the Stars and Stripes. The account that has survived through the years, undoubtedly because of its appeal although questioned by historians, is the story of Betsy Ross.

Congress appointed a committee of three—George Washington, Robert Morris and Colonel George Ross—who were charged with the responsibility of designing a national flag. The year was 1776, and by May or June the original draft was completed. At the suggestion of Colonel Ross, it was taken to the home of Elizabeth Ross, widow of his nephew, to be reproduced from the original drawing. Mrs. Ross was an expert seamstress and upholsterer, and according to the story, she copied the sketch exactly, with one exception—at her suggestion "the number of points on each star was changed from six to five."

It may be artistic license to say that Betsy Ross made the original flag, but through the years poems have been written in her honor. Indeed, the United States government once issued a beautiful stamp to commemorate "the two hundredth year of the birth of Betsy Ross, maker of the first American flag." In Philadephia, the "flag house" itself is located at 239 Arch Street where each year thousands of schoolchildren come to see the home of the first American flag.

June 14, 1777, is the true birthday of the American flag. It was on this date that George Washington presented the new flag, in person, to the Continental Congress in Philadelphia. It was on this date that the following resolution was adopted:

"Resolved, That the flag of the United States be thirteen stripes, alternate red and white; that the union be thirteen stars, white in a blue field, representing a new constellation."

When we look at our flag, with its stars and stripes and its red and its white and its blue, we might ask ourselves, "What does the flag as a whole represent?" It is said that General Washington once described the flag by saying, "We take the stars from heaven, the red from the Mother Country, separating it by white stripes, thus showing that we have separated from her; and the white stripes shall go down to posterity representing liberty." Every part and every color of the flag has a world of meaning, and each citizen should be familiar with the stories they have to tell.

FIRST UNITED STATES FLAG

The thirteen red and white stripes symbolize the thirteen Colonies that stood side by side and fought for freedom. The Flag has seven red stripes and six white. The selection was made in order to enclose or encompass the outside with red to make it easier to see at sea or at a distance.

The thirteen stars in the original flag were placed in a circle on a sky-blue field to signify that the Union would be without end; also to symbolize the equality of the states. As the nation has grown in size, so have the stars in the flag increased in number, a star being added for each new state in the Union. Each star—fifty in all—has a story to tell of hardship and danger to win a state from the wilderness and present it to the Union.

Colonel James A. Moss, United States Army (Retired), in his book *The Flag of the United States*, has described the significance of the colors as follows:

Red Is for Courage

The red in the flag proclaims the courage which the men of our race have always shown, the courage that inspires men to face danger and to do what is right. When we look at those red stripes, we recall the thousands of courageous deeds which have been done under our flag. There is hardly a spot in this broad land which does not bear silent witness to some heroic deed over which the American flag has flown. There is not a sea on the globe on which our flag has not been unfurled over men who feared no one and hesitated at nothing when honor and duty called them to the task. At home, victories of peace have often been much greater than those of war. Certainly they have required as much courage on the part of those who have carried the flag, and they have been victories which have counted heavily in making the country what it is.

White for Liberty

The white stripes in our flag mark it as the emblem of the land of the free, the country to which the oppressed of all the world may come and enjoy equality and liberty. They also tell the glorious story of patriotic men and women, who after the Civil War, joined hands for the second time in the history of our country to reunite it and make it greater than it had ever been.

Blue for Loyalty

The blue on our flag stands for loyalty. It is the blue of the heavens, the true blue. It tells the story of thousands of men and women who have been loyal to their country through thick and thin, through suffering and hardship—of men and women who

71

have hesitated at no sacrifice, even of their lives, when their country has demanded it of them.

Description of the Flag

The flag of the United States has thirteen horizontal stripes—seven red and six white—the red and white stripes alternating, and a union consisting of white stars of five points on a blue field placed on the upper quarter next to the staff and extending to the lower edge of the fourth red stripe from the top.

The number of stars is the same as the number of states in the Union.

The canton or union ("blue field") now contains fifty stars arranged in nine rows, alternating with six stars in one row and five in the other. The stars are placed with one point upward.

The proportions of the flag, as prescribed by Executive Order of President Taft, October 29, 1912, are as follows:

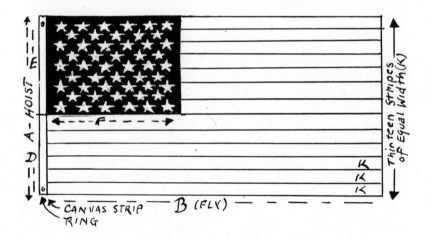

Hoist (width of flag)	1.0
Fly (length of flag)	1.9
Hoist (width of union)	7/13
Fly (length of union)	0.76
Width of each stripe	1/13
Diameter of each star	0.0616

How to Display the Flag

The United States government has enacted no laws regarding the manner of displaying and saluting the flag. However, a Flag Code was adopted by the National Flag Conference held in Washington on June 14-15, 1923, and these rules are generally accepted by everyone. The following text is based on this code:

1. *Displayed from sunrise to sunset.* It is universal custom to display the flag only from sunrise to sunset on buildings and on stationary flagstaffs in the open.

2. *Occasions on which displayed.* The flag should be displayed on national and state holidays and on historic and special occasions. It is suggested that the flag be flown on the following occasions:

> February 12—Lincoln's Birthday
> February 22—Washington's Birthday
> Second Sunday in May—Mother's Day
> May 30—Memorial Day (half-staff until noon, full staff from noon to sunset)
> June 14—Flag Day
> July 4—Independence Day
> First Monday in September—Labor Day
> October 12—Columbus Day
> First Tuesday in November—Election Day
> November 11—Veterans Day
> Last Thursday in November—Thanksgiving Day

To indicate mourning, the flag is flown at half-staff as shown below:

NOTE. When flown at half-staff, the flag should be hoisted to the peak for an instant and then lowered to the half-staff position. Before being lowered for the day, the flag should be raised again to the peak.

3. *Raising and lowering.* The flag should always be raised briskly and lowered slowly and ceremoniously.

4. *Never to touch ground.* In lowering or raising the flag, it must never be allowed to touch the ground.

5. *Never drape flag.* The flag of the United States is a national emblem which should not be draped. Drape with red, white and blue bunting, but not with the flag.

6. *How to fold a flag.* In the army or camps where the flag is raised and lowered each day as the bugle plays reveille and retreat, the flag is received by the color guard who sees that no part of it touches the ground. It is usual to fold it in half (horizontally) and then in fourths. Beginning at the striped end, the lower corner is brought up to a point to form a triangle. Continue the folding, over and over, until the entire flag becomes one blue triangle.

7. When the flag is displayed against a wall with another emblem and their staffs crossed, the United States flag is on the observer's left, and its staff in front of the other flag.

THE UNITED STATES FLAG IS AT THE CENTER OR AT THE HIGHEST POINT OF THE GROUP.

74

8. When the flag is displayed either horizontally or vertically against a wall, in a show window or elsewhere, the blue field is uppermost and to the flag's own right—that is, to the observer's left.

9. When the United States flag and flags of other nations, states

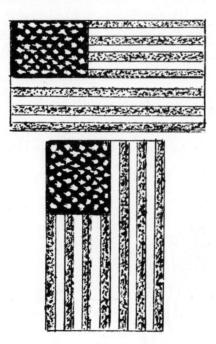

or cities, or pennants of societies are flown in this country from adjacent staffs, the United States flag is on the right of the line—that is, on the observer's left.

NOTES

A. When the United States flag and flags of other nations, states or cities or pennants of societies are flown from the adjacent staffs, the United States flag is hoisted first and lowered last.
B. When flown with flags of other nations, all staffs should be the same height and the flags of approximately equal size.
C. International usage forbids the display of the flag of one nation above that of another nation in time of peace.

10. From a staff projecting horizontally or at an angle from the window sill, balcony or front of building, the blue field goes clear to the peak.

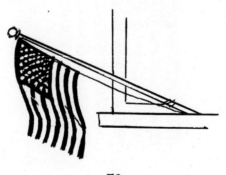

A Toast to the Flag

by George B. Harper

Here's to the RED of it,
There's not a thread of it
In all the spread of it
From foot to head
But heroes bled for it,
Faced steel and lead for it
Slipe with the dead for it,
Bathing in red.

Here's to the WHITE of it,
Who knows the might of it,
But thrills to the sight of it
Through day and night.
Womanhood's care for it
Made manhood dare for it,
Purity's prayer for it
Kept it so white.

Here's to the BLUE of it
Heavenly hue of it,
Star-spangled view of it,
Constant and true.
Here's to the WHOLE of it,
Stars, Stripes and Pole of it,
Here's to the SOUL of it
RED, WHITE and BLUE.

Pledge of Allegiance to the United States Flag

"I pledge allegiance to the flag of the United States of America and to the Republic for which it stands, one nation under God, indivisible, with liberty and justice for all."

77

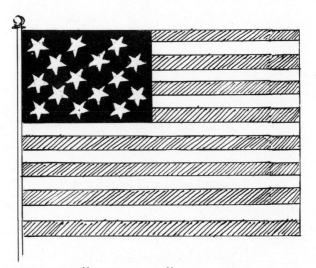

The Star Spangled Banner

The Star Spangled Banner was made immortal by Francis Scott Key, author of our national anthem. It is presumed the banner was ordered by Colonel Armistead who was in command of Fort McHenry during the War of 1812. This flag measured thirty by forty-two feet and is the only United States flag in existence with fifteen stripes. Records show that Mrs. Mary Pickersgill and her daughter of Baltimore made the flag, and for this they were paid the sum of $409.90.

It was during the Second War of Independence on the night of September 14, 1814, that Francis Scott Key paced the deck of the British battleship *Minden* during the battle for Baltimore. He had gone to see the British fleet commander to plead for the release of his friend, Dr. William Beanes. Although his request had been granted, they were detained during the attack which lasted all that day and throughout the night. Key witnessed the bombardment of Fort McHenry all night as he paced up and down the deck; and when the firing ceased at daybreak, he saw the gallant flag still waving above Fort McHenry! The sight inspired him to write "The Star Spangled Banner" and the poem was first published in the Baltimore *American*. It was later set to the tune of "Anacreon in Heaven," by John Stafford Smith. In March, 1931, it was sung by the House of Representatives after it had officially adopted it as our national anthem.

The Star Spangled Banner had eleven holes in its background and a single star missing after the battle. However, it was restored by expert needlewomen and is now in the Smithsonian Institution, Washington, D.C. It was presented by Eban Appleton, grandson of the Fort's successful defender, Colonel Armistead.

A Connecticut Flag

During the Civil War, a regiment—The Sixteenth Connecticut—after several days of hard fighting, was compelled to surrender. Seeing that surrender was inevitable, just before the enemy began to stream over the breastworks the Union soldiers had defended so bravely, the colonel of the regiment shouted: "Boys, save the colors! Don't let them fall into the enemy's hands!"

The flag was immediately stripped from its staff and cut into small pieces which were distributed among the soldiers who hid them on their persons.

The entire regiment of some five hundred men were captured and sent to a Confederate prison where nearly all of them remained until the end of the war. Each man who had a piece of the flag secretly preserved it and when a soldier died, his piece was secretly entrusted to a comrade.

At the close of the war, the regiment was released from the prison and the men returned to their homes, each still having with him the fragment of "Old Glory" that had been entrusted to his keeping. All the worn fragments were then sewn together and the old flag is now carefully preserved in the State House in Hartford, the capital of Connecticut.

One of the worst defeats suffered by the United States in the War of 1812 was the loss of the *Chesapeake* to the *Shannon*. It was then that Captain James Lawrence uttered the immortal words, "Don't give up the ship." Three months later Admiral Perry entered Put-In-Bay on Lake Erie and hoisted a special flag

from the main mast of his flagship, the *Lawrence*. It was a large blue banner and across it in white letters was the dead captain's orders, "Don't give up the ship." When the *Lawrence* was sunk in battle, Perry transferred the flag to the *Niagara* and from there he directed the final victory over the British fleet. The flag is now preserved in the Naval Academy Museum.

The Story of "Old Glory"

A century or so ago—'twas on March 17, 1821—in Salem, Massachusetts, upon the occasion of the celebration of his twenty-first birthday, William Driver, whose heart and soul were in his occupation of sailing the seas, was presented by his mother and a group of Salem girls with a beautiful American flag they had made for him. "I name her Old Glory," said he, in response to the greetings of the givers—and thus it was that the name "Old Glory" made its advent into the history of our country. From that day on "Old Glory" accompanied William Driver whenever he went to sea, and many were the notable voyages made under its flying folds including twice around the world, once around Australia and several cruises among the Archipelago Islands.

When, in 1837, Captain Driver quit the sea and settled in Nashville, Tennessee, as usual "Old Glory" accompanied him. On occasions such as Washington's birthday, the Fourth of July, and St. Patrick's Day (also the anniversary of Captain Driver's birthday) "Old Glory" could be seen gracefully waving from a rope extending from the captain's house to a tree across the street.

However, when in 1861 Tennessee seceded from the Union and hostilities began, "Old Glory" mysteriously vanished.

The morning of February 25, 1862, Union soldiers entered Nashville and took possession of the city. On that morning Captain Driver, accompanied by Captain Thatcher of the Sixth Ohio Regiment and several soldiers, came home, and calling his daughter, Mary Jane, asked her to help him rip a bedcover he was holding. And lo and behold! as the comforter was ripped apart, there was "Old Glory," which for safekeeping had been sewn between the folds of the cover when Tennessee had seceded and the American flags were objects of attacks in Nashville. At the sight of "Old Glory" the soldiers cheered, and then helped fold the flag, which Captain Driver took in his arms as the party left for the State House. As the captain climbed to the dome of the building and raised "Old Glory" over the Capitol, he exclaimed, "Thank God! I have lived to raise 'Old Glory' on the dome of the Capitol of Tennessee; I am now ready to die and go to my forefathers."

One day, not long before the good old captain went to his forefathers, he placed in the arms of his daughter a bundle, saying:

"Mary Jane, this is my old ship flag, 'Old Glory.' It has been my constant companion on many voyages. I love it as a mother loves her child; take it and cherish it as I have cherished it, for it has been my steadfast friend and protector in all parts of the world, among savage, heathen, and civilized. Keep it always."

The flag was kept and guarded as a precious heirloom in the Driver family until 1922 when it was sent to the Smithsonian Institution in Washington, where, carefully, carefully preserved under glass, surrounded by other priceless relics of the nation, in silent eloquence it now tells to us today, as it will to posterity, the beautiful story of "Old Glory."

Liberty Flag

This is one of the earliest flags on record. It was first flown in 1775 in the South and at first had a single white crescent in the

upper right-hand corner on a blue background. A year later, the word *Liberty* was added.

This was the flag that Sergeant Jasper so gallantly rescued on June 28, 1776, when the British fleet attacked Fort Sullivan at Charleston, North Carolina. When, in recognition of his gallantry, the governor presented him with his own sword and offered him a lieutenant's commission, the sergeant, who could not read or write, declined the promotion, saying, "Sir, I am not fit to keep the company of officers."

General Scott and the Stars and Stripes

One day a German appeared at General Scott's office and said he had been commissioned by a house in New York to present to him a small silk banner. It was very handsome, made of a single piece of silk, and stamped with stars and stripes in their proper colors. No doubt this was one of the first flags that had the stars and stripes either woven into or stamped onto material instead of being different pieces stitched together. The general was highly pleased and assured the donors the flag should hang in his room wherever he went, and finally enshroud him when he died.

As soon as the man departed, the general asked that the stars be counted to see if all the states were represented and the answer came that *"All* were there!" He then ordered that the flag be draped between the windows over the lounge—his favorite resting place. After the war, the same banner went with him in his berth to Europe and, true to his promise, it enveloped his coffin when he was interred at West Point.

Before the stars and stripes were incorporated into the United States flag, different sections of the country made flags from their own designs. This is quite understandable because it is a world-wide custom to carry a banner of some sort in battle, or to identify a ship at sea. In July, 1775, General Israel Putnam raised a flag over his troops upon which was inscribed the motto *"Qui trans-tulit sustinet,"* the other side bearing the words, "An Appeal to Heaven."

The Virginia troops bore a flag showing a rattlesnake coiled ready to strike and underneath were the words: "Don't tread on me." The rattlesnake became the favorite emblem with the Continental Army and Navy and sometimes the reptile was shown in thirteen parts or joints, each bearing the initial of one of the colonies.

TWO NEW STATE FLAGS

Alaska

The Alaskan emblem had its beginning in 1927, when Governor George A. Parks held a flag contest open to all Alaskan schoolchildren. It was won by Benny Benson, then thirteen, and a resident of the Jesse Lee Mission Home. His design consisted of eight gold stars placed like those in the Big Dipper and underneath was written:

The blue field is for the Alaskan sky and the forget-me-not, an Alaskan flower.

The North Star is for the future state of Alaska, the most northerly of the Union.

The dipper is for the Great Bear, symbolizing strength.

Benny Benson's design was incorporated into the official flag of Alaska in May, 1927. The act stated: ". . . that the design of the official flag is eight gold stars in a field of blue, so selected for its simplicity, its originality and its symbolism. The blue, one of our national colors, typifies the evening sky, the blue of the sea and

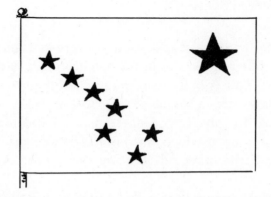

of the mountain lakes, and of wildflowers that grow in the Alaskan soil, the gold being significant of the wealth that lies hidden in Alaska's hills and streams.

"The stars, seven of which form the constellation Ursa Major, the Great Bear, the most conspicuous constellation in the Northern sky, contain the stars which form the 'Dipper,' including the 'Pointers' which point toward the eighth star in the flag, Polaris, the North Star, the ever-constant star for the mariner, the explorer, hunter, trapper, prospector, woodsman, and the surveyor. For Alaska the northernmost star in the galaxy of stars and which at some future time will take its place as the forty-ninth star in our national emblem."

In order to acquaint the children of Alaska with their new flag, the Territorial Commissioner of Education sent each student a small flag together with a poem written by Marie Drake, Deputy Commissioner:

Alaska's Flag

Eight stars of gold on a field of blue—
Alaska's flag. May it mean to you
The blue of the sea, the evening sky,
The mountain lakes, the flowers nearby;
The gold of the early sourdough's dreams,
The precious gold of the hills and streams;
The brilliant stars in the northern sky,

The "Bear"—the "Dipper"—and, shining high
The great North Star with its steady light,
Over land and sea a beacon bright,
Alaska's flag—to Alaska dear,
The simple flag of a last frontier.

This poem was later set to music by Mrs. Eleanor Dusenbury and was published in 1940.

NOTE. When the legislature accepted Benny Benson's design for its official banner, it appropriated $1,000 to send him to Washington, D.C., to present a flag to President Coolidge. However, the trip failed to materialize and the money was later used for his education.

Hawaiian Flag

The Hawaiian flag shows the influence of the British Union Flag which was planted on the islands by Captain James Cook in 1778. The banner shown in the drawing was adopted by the territorial government in 1925. To describe it: "On a blue canton are the combined three British Union crosses—St. George, St. Andrew and St. Patrick. The eight stripes of red, white and blue in the field represent the eight main islands in the Hawaiian group."

Aloha Oe

(Composed by Queen Libuokalani at Manuawili, Hawaii, in 1878.
Manuscript copy in Hawaii Public Archives)

1. Proudly sweep the rain by the cliffs,
    As on it glides through the trees;
  Still following ever the liko
    The A—hi-hi le-hu of the vale.

  Chorus
  Farewell to thee, farewell to thee,
    Thou charming one who dwells in shaded bowers,
  Farewell to thee, farewell to thee,
    One fond embrace e'er I depart
  Until we meet again.

2. Thus sweet memories come back to me
    Bring fresh remembrance of the past,
  Dearest one, yes, though not my own
    From thee true love shall ne'er depart.

3. I have seen and watched thy loveliness,
    Thou sweet Rose of Maunawii,
  And 'tis there the birds oft love to dwell
    And sip the honey from thy lips.

The United States Flag

by Calvin Coolidge

Works which endure come from the soul of the people. The mighty in their pride walk alone to destruction. The humble walk hand in hand with Providence to immortality. Their work survives. When the people of the Colonies were defending their liberties against the might of kings, they chose their banner from the design set in the firmament through all eternity. The flags of the great empires of that day are gone, but the Stars and Stripes remain. It pictures the vision of a people whose eyes were turned to the rising dawn. It represents the hope of a father for his posterity. It was never flaunted for the glory of royalty, but to be born under it is to be a child of a king and to establish a home under it is to be the founder of a royal house. Alone of all flags it expresses the sovereignty of the people which endures when all else passes away. Speaking with their voice it has the sanctity of revelation. He who lives under it and is loyal to it is loyal to truth and justice everywhere. He who lives under it and is disloyal to it is a traitor to the human race everywhere. What could be saved if the flag of the American nation were to perish?

Bibliography

David Eggenberger, *Flags of the United States* (New York: Thomas Y. Crowell, 1959).

Colonel James A. Moss, *The Flag of the United States* (Washington, D.C.: United States Flag Association, 1933).

CIVIL WAR FLAG

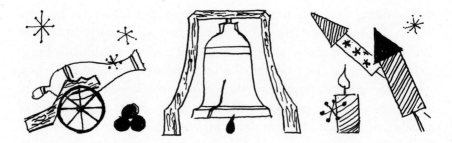

9. INDEPENDENCE DAY—JULY 4

This is our grand national holiday—the Glorious Fourth—when all Americans manifest their patriotic enthusiasms in various ways.

The army marks the day by firing a salute of thirteen guns and reading the Declaration of Independence. All over the country, church bells are rung in memory of the Liberty Bell that proclaimed our independence. This most famous bell, by the way, was made in England and around its rim are these prophetic words:

> "Proclaim Liberty throughout the land
> unto all the inhabitants thereof."

On the day the Declaration of Independence was signed, crowds began to gather around Independence Hall, and at 2:00 P.M., a boy ran into the street shouting: "Ring! Ring! Ring! It was four days later that John Nixon read the Declaration of Independence on the square of Philadelphia and then went to the Commons where it was declared again before the five battalions stationed there. The crowd went wild with joy—the King's Arms were taken down from the Court House—and everywhere people pledged allegiance to their new country. It was a beautiful star-lit evening, bonfires were lighted, people paraded and danced in the streets, and there were fireworks. . . .

July 4 is still celebrated in much the same fashion—there are parades, dancing, fireworks—only the firecrackers are missing. Since it falls in the summertime, it is our most gala holiday when parents can take their families on outings, either into the country or along the seashore. For this reason, we decided to suggest a "Patriotic Shindig" for a Fourth of July entertainment. The word "shindig" implies gay entertainment with feasting and dancing—and, we are going to add, "in the country." We offer no set program—just a number of activities that may help in planning such a celebration.

PATRIOTIC SHINDIG

Since it is easier to plan a small party than a big one, we are suggesting activities suitable for a large group participation. It is assumed that a picnic ground or a park area will be available for a neighborhood gathering, and the shindig can be organized and supervised by professional group leadership from the community. We have only enough space in this chapter to suggest ways to feed the people and keep them merry.

Games

Just to keep the celebration in tune with the Fourth, here are some games our forefathers played during the time of the Revolution:

Pioneer Game Equipment. The drawing on page 91 shows primitive play equipment found on village squares or commons, comparable to our playgrounds today. It would require no great engineering feat or outlay of money to build some of it and have it available for the children. It might be very amusing to see their reactions after playing on jungle gyms, slides, seesaws, etc.

A Game for Men. A ball is one of the oldest pieces of game equipment, but it has not always been carried in the arms or hit with a bat. Football, for instance, has been played for several hundred years, but kicked, not carried. In certain parts of New England, particularly on Shrove Tuesdays, there were great contests among the men in the villages. Sometimes the married men turned out against the bachelors, or sometimes there was a battle royal between the "Upwards" and "Downwards" in which the whole crowd took part.

The game resembled football, only the goals were miles apart; perhaps one might be a bridge and another a hill top. It was played with a round ball which was kicked, and needless to say the game was rough. If the game were played at a shindig, modern football rules might be injected, and there would be fun for all.

Torpedoes. Give each player six horse chestnuts or buckeyes that have been painted to resemble torpedoes that used to be thrown on July 4.

The game is best played against a wall or the side of a house; but choose a spot where there is no grown person who will be annoyed with the noise. A foot or two from the wall place a hat or a basket. Then let each participant try to aim his buckeye at the wall in such a way that it will rebound and fall into the basket. Each one placed in the basket wins a point. After a little practice players will be able to run up quite a score. Place a bottle or a small pan on a fence. See who is the best marksman. The ringing sound of the glass or tin will tell plainly whenever the bull's-eye is hit.

Pick Up Sticks for the very young should be added to the list of games. Jack Straws is another name for it. Cut any number of sticks of wood ½" x ½" x 14" and paint them three different colors —red, white and blue. Throw them in a basket and ask the children to remove one without disturbing the other sticks. Make up rules, according to the age of the children.

Games of individual skills are always popular at the shindig. A shooting gallery, for instance, weight lifting, wrestling—anything that will entertain an audience. A very simple contest that requires only a baseball for equipment is to draw a circle on the ground three feet in diameter and see if anyone can stand at the edge, throw the ball straight up into the air, and have it land back into the circle.

PIONEER GAME EQUIPMENT

Buffoons

A buffoon stage can easily be the biggest attraction at a shin-dig. It offers an opportunity for impromptu dramatics that can continue all during the day. If the stage is to be out-of-doors, place it on the edge of the grounds so the people taking the part of the buffoons cannot be observed from the rear.

The stage, in general, consists of a wooden frame on standards and covered with a dark cloth, either black or navy blue. It should be at least six feet tall and eight feet wide. Cut two holes large enough for a head to push through and high enough up for the person to stand behind the screen at the same time. (Children can stand on stools.) On either side of the buffoon body, cut two more holes for arms to enter the sleeves. Make the bodies about sixteen inches tall and put weights of some kind in their feet so they will stand erect. Fasten a string eight inches long to each toe of the shoes and tie a small ring to the other. This will be used as a device to animate the body. Slip a ring over each forefinger and move the hands in a rhythm to suit the story being dramatized.

When the buffoons are to be used at a large gathering, dress them in simple men's and women's costumes. You can have a number of hats on hand and indicate various characters by a change of headdress. We suggest a raccoon cap and a sunbonnet be used at a patriotic shindig, or if the story demands it, a cocked hat and one with plumes. If youngsters want to act as buffoons, it is easy to substitute other bodies in the front of the stage that are dressed in children's clothes.

Persons talented in ad-libbing can entertain the crowd by carrying on amusing conversations. Many of our folk songs tell a story about a boy and girl; they are excellent for this type of production—particularly if there is dialogue answering back and forth. The song "Soldier, Soldier, Will You Marry Me" given on page 94 is a good example. It is well to have a narrow shelf across the center of the stage at a point where the buffoon's feet rest to hold stage properties such as are mentioned in the song. And don't forget, the children will want to dramatize nursery rhymes; so bring along some properties for them.

Outdoor Picture Studio

One of the charms the buffoon stage will have at the shindig is the background it will provide for everyone wishing to have his picture taken. Young and old alike will enjoy poking their heads through the hole, donning a headdress and smiling at the cameraman. With this in mind, try to locate the stage at a place where the sun's rays will come from the right direction for taking a photograph. This, by the way, is a good way to raise money—charge a small fee and have your own cameraman.

SOLDIER, SOLDIER, WILL YOU MARRY ME?

2. Soldier, soldier, will you
    marry me? etc.
   When I have no shoes to
    put on.
   Then she ran away to the
    shoemaker's shop, etc.

3. Soldier, soldier, will you
    marry me? etc.
   When I have no hat to put
    on.
   Then she ran away to the
    hatter's shop, etc.

4. Soldier, soldier, will you
    marry me? etc.
   When I have no gloves to
    put on.
   So she ran away to a glove-
    maker's shop, etc.

5. Soldier, soldier, will you
    marry me? etc.
   "Oh, how can I marry such
    a pretty maid as thee,
   When I've got a good wife
    at home?"

Two children are selected to play the parts. The little girl sings the first half of the verse and the little boy the second half. When he says he has no coat to put on, she borrows one from some other one of the children and so on for each verse. The last verse, which is sung by the soldier alone, always creates great merriment.

Outdoor Cooking

When one goes to a large party, eating is half the fun. The food that will be enjoyed most at a shindig is the kind where the raw materials are brought along and cooked over an open fire. The outdoor dishes we are going to describe usually require a long period of cooking, so it is well to prepare some sandwiches or light food to be eaten several hours before dinner. Let's begin with an open-air snack bar:

Open-Air Snack Bar

Place several tables or build a booth underneath a shady tree for the purpose of holding the necessary utensils and ingredients. Arrange for all the drinks to be served from one place apart from the other refreshments, and have plenty of cans handy to receive the used paper cups. Suspend a barrel hoop from one of the tree limbs to hold meat for the sandwiches as shown in the drawing. This might include a small ham, bologna, dried beef and other cold cuts. Use double hooks over the hoop so the pieces can easily be taken down and put back again.

A cracker barrel would add to the Fourth of July atmosphere— also a round of store cheese. Be sure to close the bar early enough to keep up hearty appetites for supper.

A Burgoo

A hundred years ago the men of Kentucky, in celebration of a holiday, would get up what they called a burgoo. Early in the morning the party would meet at the appointed place and decide what each should contribute toward the making of this most delectable stew. Those who were fond of hunting would go forth in search of birds, squirrels, rabbits and game of all kinds, with which the woods were filled. Some caught fish, and others provided fowl, pork, vegetables and condiments.

As the ingredients were brought in, those who had charge of the cooking prepared and dropped them into an immense pot which, half full of water, was suspended over a roaring fire. When everything of which the stew was composed was cooked into shreds, the burgoo was pronounced done. It was served in tin cups and eaten with shell spoons made by splitting a stick and wedging a mussel shell in the opening.

Burgoo Stew

Use two pounds of salt pork; the same of lean beef; two good-sized chickens, or fowl of any kind; two quarts of oysters, the same of clams; twelve potatoes, four turnips, one onion, two quarts of tomatoes and any other vegetables which may be obtainable. Make a bouquet of parsley, celery and a very little bay leaf, thyme and hyssop, tied together with thread.

96

Put the beef, fowl, pork, oysters, clams and a handful of salt in a large iron kettle, three-quarters full of water; skim it before it begins to boil hard, and add the other ingredients; keep the kettle covered and boil until the bones fall apart from the meat. Serve hot with crackers or corn bread. The cooking time is from five to seven hours.

A more modern recipe for burgoo is to put two pounds of shank beef, with a bone, a half pound of baby lamb and a medium-sized chicken into a pot, with water, salt, black pepper and one pod of red pepper. The vegetables are the same, except that two cups of fresh cut corn are added.

Ember Cooking

This kind of cooking is based on a plan whereby every individual does his own cooking over a bed of glowing embers. Each person also supplies his own equipment and usually his own food. This is an excellent way to have food served at a shindig where there is no central food committee and no money to advance for supplies. The community part of the project is to build fires and keep them burning until there are several inches of coals for the cooking.

First of all, dig a round pit several feet in diameter, two or three in depth, and line it with medium-sized stones. Be sure the stones are dry—water-soaked stones are apt to explode in the fire. Also, line the pit with more stones to prevent the fire from spreading. You will need several pits to accommodate a large crowd, as each individual should be able to cook near the center where the embers are the hottest. Pile the pit high with hard wood, light the fire and keep it burning several hours until there are several inches of hot coals. The rocks in the bottom will help retain heat and keep the embers alive for cooking.

When it comes to a choice of foods for cooking, the easiest procedure is to bring a complete dinner wrapped in aluminum foil, place it on the coals and keep turning it until the food is cooked. But it is more fun to try some primitive methods not practiced at home:

Fish in bags. Select a portion of fish filet (any kind of fish.) that is not over a half inch thick. Place it on a piece of waxed paper and pour over some melted butter and salt and pepper to taste. Add lemon juice if you like.

Now wrap around it several layers of wet newspapers and then put it in a wet paper bag. You need not soak the paper ahead of time, just have a bucket of water handy and dip it in and out. Place the package on the bed of embers and keep turning it from time to time just often enough to keep the bag from burning. The principle is to allow the fish to steam long enough to cook. It will take twenty-five or thirty minutes.

Individual pressure cookers can be made out of coffee tins. Line the bottom of the tin with two strips of bacon and cover the top with finely chopped onions. Add next a layer of hamburger that has been seasoned to taste and on top put any vegetables (in medium-sized pieces) you like—carrots, celery, potatoes, etc., and add salt and pepper. Fill any space remaining in the can with crushed wax paper and put the lid on your cooker.

Water must be added either at the beginning or a little later— that is, if you want the meat and juice to be brown. Set the can down into the embers and check the contents from time to time. The lid will not fit tightly enough to cause an explosion but it does add some pressure to the cooking. The cooking period will be about thirty minutes.

Cooking in a popcorn shaker is a good method for young children who are too small to indulge in stick cooking. They can cook almost any type of food in a popcorn shaker—frankfurters, hamburgers, etc., and—if the bottom is lined with a piece of tin—fry eggs or potatoes.

Biscuit twists. A good addition to an ember-cooked meal would be biscuit twists made on a stick. Select a stick ¾ inch in diameter and remove about six inches of bark from the better end. Put a cup of biscuit mixture in a paper bag, moisten it with a little milk and wrap the dough around the stick. Cook the twist slowly over the embers and remove it from the stick while it is still hot. Fill the center with fruit or jam.

Square Dancing

We can think of no better way to end a patriotic shindig than an evening of dancing. The folk type of dance would best suit the theme and your public library no doubt has a number of books on the subject. Here are a few with a patriotic connotation just to get you started:

Your Land And My Land

Your land and my land will be our land some day;

Bright bars and white stars lead-ing both on our way.

One flag for ev-er___ when war and hat-red have gone, So!

Glo-ry, glo-ry hal-le-lu-jah! We'll sing as we go march-ing on! Hoo-ray! (*shouted*)

Formation. Partners in circle formation all around room, facing in line of direction.

Four walking steps forward—2 measures.

Face partners and do a tap step (step on left heel and rock forward, bring the right foot back to left heel, step forward again with left foot, turn half right on ball of foot and repeat the step in opposite direction).

Four walking steps forward—2 measures.

Face partner and do the tap step again as described above except on last count and do not turn again to line of direction, but remain facing partner—2 measures.

Give right hand to partner and grand right and left until reaching the third partner (counting your present partner as No. 1), give military salute on the word "So!"—4 measures.

Give right hand to that partner and turn around with skipping steps—5 measures.

Stamp three times—2 measures.

Shout "Hooray!" and wave right hand—1 measure.

LOG CABIN (SINGING CALL)

Introduction

1. We will all join hands and circle to the left.
   To the little old log cabin in the lane.
2. We are all going wrong, turn and go the other way,
   To the little old log cabin in the lane.

100

3. Your places all and balance all and everybody swing,
   To the little old log cabin in the lane.

Quadrilles

4. Then it's left hand to the corner, and right hand to your own;
   The grand chain all the way around.
   (Repeat chorus music for Call 5-6)
5. Take the first one by the left hand, the next one by the right,
   To the little old log cabin in the lane;
6. And when you meet your partner, you promenade around,
   To the little old log cabin in the lane.

Change Call (for each couple)

(Repeat Music and Verse for each 4 lines.)
7. First couple to the right, you change and you swing,
   To the little old log cabin in the lane;
8. And now you take that lady and waltz her twice around,
   To the little old log cabin in the lane.
9. You lead right on, you change and you swing,
   To the little old log cabin in the lane;
10. And now you take that lady and waltz her twice around,
    To the little old log cabin in the lane.
11. You lead right on, you change and you swing,
    To the little old log cabin in the lane;
12. And now you take that lady and waltz her right back home.
    To that little old lob cabin in the lane.

Chorus Call

13. Your places all and balance all, and everybody swing,
    To the little old log cabin in the lane;
14. Then it's left hand to the corner, right hand to your own,
    And grand chain all the way around.
15. Take the first one by the left hand and the next one by the right,
    To the little old log cabin in the lane;
16. And when you meet your partner, you promenade around,
    To the little old log cabin in the lane.

Log Cabin

Chorus

Dixie

(Music: *Dixie*)

Formation. Single circle.

Circle: With shuffle step, circle to right—8 measures.

Cake Walk: Gentlemen, let loose of lady's hand on your right, still holding hand of lady on left, step out in front of her (which reverses your direction) and cake walk—8 measures; face partners at finish.

Gentlemen dance round: Passing partner on her left—gentlemen dance complete circle—4 measures.

Lady dances round: Passing the gentleman on his right; lady dances, complete circle—4 measures.

Glide: Join both hands and glide to gentleman's left, 3 slow glides—3 measures.

Stamp: To words "In Dixie" stamp 3 times—1 measure.

Glide: Still holding hands, 2 slow glides in opposite direction.

Circle Round: Join right hands and circle three-quarter way round, coming into single circle—1 measure.

Bow: All bow centerward—1 measure.

Yankee Doodle

Formation: Large circle, boys on left.

(1) All join hands and march around counter-clockwise, while verse is being sung.

(2) Partners face. On first measure of chorus, all join hands and take two slip-steps counter-clockwise, and on second measure two slip steps back.

(3) In the last two measures, all couples swing each other going to the right.

4) Boys move on to the next girl, counter-clockwise.

Repeat until boy gets back to partner.

A Doorstep Patriotic Party

Here are some suggestions for a Doorstep party that may be given any time during the summer. After all, a party can have a patriotic theme even though it is not given on a holiday.

Invitations. Music is an essential element in any party; so in writing your invitations, ask your guests to compose a song of two or three stanzas that can be sung to familiar tunes such as "Rally Round the Flag Boys!" or "Yankee Doodle." They should bring them along to the party together with a number of copies of the words so everyone can join in the singing. Give a prize to the one that is most original or clever.

Decorations. Of course, you will want to use flags and red, white and blue bunting or, if the party is given on July 4, the colonial colors, blue and buff. We should like to suggest you use some novel mobiles that can be suspended from the ceiling of the porch:

Patriotic Mobiles

A mobile means "to move" and is built on the principle of perfect weight and balance. Consider carefully the illustration and note that when an object is used on one side of the string, one or two weighing the same are tied to the other.

Figure A shows a novel type of mobile made by twisting long

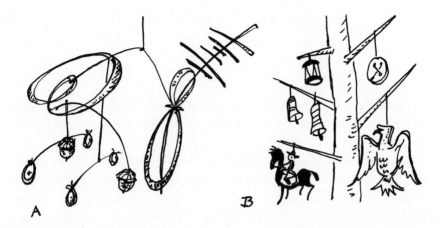

A   B

stems of vines or branches into loops and tying them into place. It makes no difference how many loops are on each side as long as they balance. Cover the open areas with red, white and blue tissue paper, and if you like, cut out patriotic symbols such as balls, firecrackers, eagles, etc., and paste them in the circles.

Figure B is the usual mobile made with a number of wooden dowels extending from a central stem. Patriotic objects, either in three dimensions or cut from paper, are suspended from them on a thin string.

The oldest type of mobile that has been used for centuries by the Chinese. It is made up of a number of long slender pieces of glass, usually decorated, that give out tinkling notes when the wind blows them together. If you can find several, or better still, make them, they will add a merry sound to your party.

Entertainment. As each guest arrives, give him a small paper shopping bag that has been decorated with patriotic motifs. In the bag will be all the materials he will need at the party. This may be a pad and pencil, copies of songs, game equipment, a lunch if you like, etc. Getting back to our theme, "A Doorstep Party," let's begin with a game that lasts off and on all evening:

Passing By. If your porch faces a street you should see a number of people or animals strolling along. Make a check list, giving points, something like this:

Woman	1	Automobile	1
Man	1	Horse	10
Baby	5	Dog	5
Bird	5	Cat	5

Butterflies. If the party is for young children, they might enjoy making butterflies to see which can make the most unusual, most beautiful, etc.

You will need scissors, toothpicks, white paper and tubes of oil paint in six different colors—red, blue, green, yellow, black and white. Each person takes a sheet of medium-thin white paper 5″ x 7″ and folds it in half. This will form the body of the butterfly. On one half of the paper put on tiny dabs of different-colored oil paints and press the two pieces together. As they are pressed faint colors begin to show through. Draw an outline of a butterfly

wing and add an antenna at one end; then cut around the outline, including both pieces of paper. Run a toothpick through the center at the bottom for a body. Ask everyone to hang their butterflies on a curtain so the best can be judged by the audience.

A hostess should never appear to be too anxious to entertain her guests each moment of the party. Let people entertain themselves. Herein is the secret of success. The entertainment might end with some informal dancing or singing, and of course some refreshments.

Patriotic Foods

A blazing dessert. Cut red apples in half, place them in a pan or pyrex plate and bake in the usual way. Remove from the oven and sprinkle brown sugar in the hollows. Broil slowly until sugar crusts. Center each with lump sugar soaked 15 or 20 minutes in lemon extract. Light lumps and bring to the table flaming.

Red and white luncheon. To complete the patriotic connotation, serve on blue dishes: tomato aspic, boiled ham and chicken, creamed potatoes, buttered beets, crab apples stuffed with cream cheese salad, pineapple ice cream with maraschino cherries.

Cupcakes can be decorated in various ways. An easy uncooked icing to make is to cream a small package of cream cheese, ⅛ pound of butter, a little salt, flavoring and any vegetable coloring you wish to use. Add one-half can of evaporated milk and thicken with powdered sugar.

An amusing decoration for cupcakes is to ice them to resemble drums. Cookies can be cut in the shape of bells and decorated with colored icing. Put the details on with a toothpick before the cookies are baked.

For Pan-American Day

Alfajores (North American way). Shake one can of condensed milk very well. Place can in a saucepan and cover completely with water. Boil rapidly for 1½ hours, adding more water as needed to keep can covered. Cool under water. It is not necessary to add vanilla unless you want to. Spread vanilla wafers with the contents of the can. Sandwich them, spread edges with filling; then roll in coconut.

We heard about a delicious South American dessert but we have no name for it. Blend chocolate and coffee ice cream in a freezing tray, and as you do it sprinkle layers of cinnamon. Refreeze.

Barbecue

Since barbecued meat is one of the popular party dishes, we decided to add a recipe for a barbecue sauce that can be used either on pork or chicken. The amounts are for twelve people:

> 1 can tomato soup
> ½ cup vinegar
> ½ teaspoon salt
> ½ cup melted butter
> 1 bottle tomato catsup
> 2 tablespoons sugar
> ½ teaspoon black pepper
> 1 grated onion
> 1 teaspoon Worcestershire sauce

Make a mop of cheesecloth and inside place a bouquet of mixed herbs.

10. COLUMBUS DAY—OCTOBER 12

Columbus Day is one of the favorite holidays in school because the story includes all the elements so appealing to children—heroism, adventure, the sea islands, storms and finally a happy ending! With this in mind, we have written a running story, including the most important events in the life of Christopher Columbus. This story a "reader" may tell in a tempo suitable for children to dramatize. This can be done either in a pantomime or a puppet show. The pantomime can be acted out on the stage, or it can be shown as shadows behind an illuminated screen. A puppet show such as the Chinese use is an excellent project for a schoolroom, as all the children can have a part in making it.

CHINESE-TYPE PUPPET SHOW

First of all, let us describe briefly the type of puppets used, how they are manipulated and the plan of the stage. Once you know the basic principles, the children can adapt it to their age group and the material they have at hand.

A   B

FIGURE 1. PUPPETS AND HOLDER

The puppet characters and any pieces of scenery that are to be used in the show are cut out of cardboard according to one scale. They are held in place by inserting each piece into a groove which has been cut along the top of a long narrow wooden stick. Figure 1A shows detail of puppet and 1B how it is fastened to the stick. The stick should be at least two feet in length and the groove a half inch deep and the same width as the thickness of the cardboard.

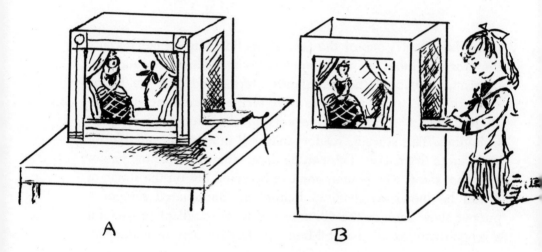

FIGURE 2. TYPES OF STAGES

The stage can be a simple boxlike frame designed to sit on a table or desk (Figure 2A), or a tall panel with an opening at the top (Figure 2B). The opening for the stage must be high enough to allow the children to either kneel or stand below it as they move the puppets across the front. It is well to have small curtains which can be drawn to indicate different acts or the passage of time. The stage can be made either of three-ply wood or cardboard, depending on whether it is to be permanent or temporary.

FIGURE 3. STAGE SCENERY

There are two ways in which one may show the setting of a play—first, a painted backdrop (Figure 3A); and second, the making of cutouts of trees, houses and other objects to be inserted in the groove between the actual characters (Figure 3B). The advantage of the latter is that the story can be told continuously without stopping for changes of scenery. If a backdrop is to be used, decorate it in as subtle colors as possible. This will allow the puppets to remain the focal point, which is important while dramatizing the story. Scenery bits cut from cardboard, such as trees or houses, should be somewhat taller than the characters but not necessarily to scale.

All puppets and parts of the scenery are cut from stiff cardboard. If they are to be used as silhouettes behind an illuminated screen, they may be used without decoration or color. However, it is more fun to use them with color as the Chinese do, who even

FIGURE 4. HOW TO MAKE PUPPETS

111

go so far as to make the clothes in finest silk and to add real hair to the heads.

The puppets and bits of scenery should all be drawn before the cutting begins so that every piece fits the same scale. The size of the figures will depend on the distance between the stage and the audience. If the children are small, the figures can be colored with crayons; otherwise, tempera colors are used because they are inexpensive as well as vivid—which makes them clearly visible from a distance.

The Production

First of all, read the story over carefully and decide which episodes in the life of Columbus can be most easily dramatized by using this type of puppet. It is not necessary to keep a running show on the stage even though the story is being read continuously during the production. In fact, it is more effective to divide the story into a number of acts, or "flashes"; the pauses will provide time for changing puppets in the carrier.

The number of sticks, or carriers, necessary to have depends on how many puppets, bits of scenery and properties are to be used in each act. The length of each carrier must be the same as the width of the opening in the stage. Also, each side of the stage opening should measure the same, in order to allow room for a full carrier on the right side ready to go on and the one in the center to pass off.

A   B

FIGURE 5. PUPPETS IN ACTION

112

Figure 5A shows puppets in place on the stage and ready for the first lines in the story. Figure 5B shows the second carrier backstage ready to follow. Keep the figures moving slowly, or allow them to remain standing, according to the action of the story. Draw the curtains between the different acts of the play or to denote the passage of time. The story follows.

How Christopher Columbus Discovered America

Christopher Columbus was born in the beautiful Italian city of Genoa on the Mediterranean seacoast. Always, as a little boy, he watched his father card wool and weave it into fabrics on a great loom. On one side of his home he could see the beautiful Alpine Mountains white with snow; but young Christopher had eyes only for the other side of his home which bordered on the Mediterranean. There he would watch the ships with their white sails and dream of what might lie beyond the sea. When he was old enough to read, his favorite stories were those which Marco Polo brought back of his adventures in the Far East. Each one of these stories made him more determined that some day he would take the same course.

When Columbus was old enough, he spent most of his time on the water, and soon he learned how to navigate a sailing vessel and manipulate the sails. A little later, when he was sixteen, he went on a long voyage to Iceland. That was the turning point in his life, for then he knew he could never be a weaver but must live with the sea.

About this time, maps came into use for navigating ships, and Columbus decided to be a mapmaker by profession. He married Relipa Moniz, the daughter of a navigator who died shortly after the marriage. In his will the navigator left all his fine instruments and charts to his son-in-law, and these enabled Columbus to become a master mapmaker. Soon he took his wife and son, Diego, to Lisbon where they lived, when not residing on some small islands, for the next twenty years. Because Columbus lived by the sea, famous navigators of that time would come to consult him and hire him to make their charts.

113

By the time Columbus was forty-six years old, he was making enough money to support three families, but he could not forget the stories of Marco Polo and his dream of finding a new way to India and the Far East. Besides, each day he would listen to "sea gossip" as told by navigators when returning from trips far out to sea: A pilot told the King of Portugal that he saw near Cape St. Vincent an unusual piece of wood floating in the water, carved with a primitive tool. Furthermore, he found large vessels capable of holding over a gallon of water or wine. Another ship had seen pines near the Azores, and since none grew there, these must have come from the West. . . .

Columbus believed the stories, and as he looked out on the sea, he began to wonder why, "when a ship departed, the hull disappeared first on the horizon and then the sails." And as he gazed at the "new" moon, he wondered if the larger part of it could be covered by the shadow of the earth. If so, could the earth be round? He began to expound his theories about the earth being round—if it were, one could sail straight ahead and eventually come back to the original starting point! But his friends only laughed and asked how he "could reach the East by sailing West."

In those days Spain was desperately looking for a new route to India over which to bring spices, perfumes and silks, so eagerly desired by women. The products had to be carried by camels over burning sands, and, worst of all, the traders often had to fight the cruel Turks.

For sixteen years Columbus tried to find someone who would believe his theory enough to finance an expedition that would chart a new course for Europe's trade. Finally, through the influence of a friend, Don Luis de Santangel, Columbus was granted an audience with Queen Isabella and King Ferdinand, who listened to his story in amazement as he said, "Your Majesties, I want to sail West and discover a new route to India. There I hope to find much gold and extend your kingdom beyond this realm." At first Ferdinand did not want to spend the money because recent wars had been so costly, but Isabella offered to sell her jewels in order that Columbus might make the trip. Fortunately,

DRAWINGS FOR PUPPETS

Columbus' friend, Don Luis de Santangel, was Minister of the Budget, and he offered to finance the expedition out of money in the treasury, plus some of his own. It was agreed that Columbus should have the title of admiral of all lands discovered and also be viceroy and governor of such lands. In addition, he was to have one-tenth of the precious stones, gold, silver and other products that might be found.

Two ships, the *Niña* and the *Santa María*, were placed under the command of Columbus, and enough money was advanced to pay the crew for four months. Later, another ship, the *Pinta*, was added to the group. This ship was owned by Martín Alonzo Pinzón, a wealthy Spaniard, who captained it during the voyage. As can well be imagined, it took more than ten weeks to load the ships for the long journey. The total number of men on board the three ships was 129; and of these, ninety-nine were crew members, the remaining twenty or thirty others included officers of the King, as well as several doctors and domestic servants. The ships' stores included:

Fresh water for the entire voyage
Every man expected a daily ration each day:
   1 lb. biscuits
   2 liters wine
   ⅜ lb. meat or fish—with now and then cheese, onions and vegetables, oil and vinegar, all necessary at sea for a period of six months.

The ships' bottoms were ballasted with ammunition, as well as stone and metal required for artillery.

Usual stores of lighting, heating, sailing and medical equipment were included; also some "gross and slight" wares fit for commerce with barbarous people—glass beads, mirrors, colored bonnets, pins and needles.

The ships were ready to sail on August 2, 1492. Columbus sailed on the *Santa Maria*, but Juan de la Cosa, the owner, was master of the crew. Nothing of importance happened until they reached the Canary Islands. There the *Pinta's* helm was broken, making it

COLUMBUS COMMEMORATIVE STAMPS

necessary to ground the ship for a month for repairs. When the ships were ready to sail again, they ran into a flat calm that kept them within sight of land for two days and nights. The sailors took this to be a warning, or bad omen, and wanted to turn back, but Columbus had made up his mind to sail due west, and nothing would induce him to change his course.

On the morning of September 9, the trade winds began to blow, and the three ships left the coast of Ferro by nightfall. Every trace of land had disappeared, and before them lay a vast expanse of unchartered ocean. From the point of view of weather, the next ten days were the "honeymoon" part of the voyage; the trade winds blew as steadily as they always do, and the sky was blue overhead. But sailing for ten days without sight of land was too much for the crew; and they began "first to beg" the Admiral to turn around, and then they planned to mutiny.

On the night of September 13, a strange thing happened, frightening the crew more than ever! The mariners noted that the compass needles pointed northwest, whereas they knew that the night before they had pointed slightly east of the North Star. Columbus realized that they were "right on the Polar Star," and from that point the needles would begin pointing toward the west. For the first time in history a ship had crossed the magnetic line—another proof that the earth was round!

On September 18 the fleet made its last twenty-four hours of good sailing weather—150 miles—and from that time on, they had wind on the stern, day after day. In six days they traveled only 380 miles. The men had nothing of importance to do, and the grumbling again assumed the proportions of mutiny. Columbus knew what was going on, but his faith had been strengthened during the past few days because he had seen several unmistakable signs of land: At dawn on the twenty-first, the sea was covered with seaweed as far as the eye could see. As the ships made way through the great tangle, several large masses of land, covered with fresh vegetation were observed, and these Columbus decided had broken away from some mainland in a storm.

Also, a large crab was seen among the seaweed—another sign

118

COLUMBUS COMMEMORATIVE STAMPS

that land was near, because a crab never ventures far from shore —and showers of rain fell without wind, almost a phenomenon when this occurred at sea.

Then Columbus began to observe great flocks of birds passing overhead, but their flight was in a southwesterly direction. He remembered that the Portuguese had discovered the outmost Azores by following a flock of birds, so he reset his course from west to southwest and followed the feathered pilots. If he had not changed his direction, he would have taken a day longer to reach the mainland.

A reward of ten thousand maravedis had been promised to the person who should first see land, and on October 11 "a fine silk doublet" had been added to the prize. During the day, the *Niña* picked up a green branch and a little flower that resembled the dog roses that grow on hedges in Castile. During the early hours that night a carved stick was seen floating in the water and a little later Columbus thought he saw a light "like a wax candle, rising and falling." But it was Rodego de Triana, on the *Pinta*, who shouted "Land! Land!" at two o'clock that morning. He saw the white sands gleaming in the moonlight and this time it was true!

At daybreak, October 12, 1492, the famous landing of Columbus took place. The boats were lowered and Columbus, with a large part of the men, went ashore. He was dressed in a most magnificent apparel and his right hand held high the royal banner of Spain. Pinzon and his brother carried the banner of the expedition on which was depicted a green cross with an *F* on one arm and a *Y* on the other, for Ferdinand and Isabella. Over the top of the letters were his and her crowns. The officers embraced Columbus or kissed his hands, while the sailors threw themselves at his feet asking forgiveness. He summoned the other captains as witnesses, erected a large cross at the mouth of the harbor, thus taking possession of the land in the name of their sovereigns. He named the islands "San Salvador."

These proceedings were watched with amazement by a multitude of men, women and children who were different from any the Spaniards had ever seen. They wore no clothes, and most of their bodies were greased or painted. Columbus saw they were gentle and peaceful people and gave them some little red caps and glass beads which they hung around their necks. In return, the men came swimming out to the boats bringing cotton thread in skeins, parrots, darts and many other things.

Columbus remained ten days to cruise among the islands, and during this time the *Pinta* deserted. The *Santa Maria* was sunk on one of the reefs, so Columbus was forced to load all on the *Niña* for the homeward voyage. The return journey was generally uneventful except for one storm that raged for four days and nights. Columbus, expecting their tiny boat to be engulfed in the waves, wrote two brief reports on parchment to Ferdinand and Isabella telling of his discoveries and the success of his Expedition. Each report was wrapped in cloth and enclosed in the middle of a large cake of wax and placed in a barrel. One barrel was cast into the sea while the other remained standing on the little quarter-deck to await the fate of the ship. Of course, we know that the little ship survived and brought them safely into the harbor of Palos at noon on March 15, 1493. As her story flew from mouth to mouth, the whole community broke forth in rejoicing, bells were rung and there was dancing in the streets!

At Court Columbus was asked to sit in the presence of the two sovereigns—a great honor—as he related the story of his journey. He showed them samples of silver, a few pearls, trinkets of gold and a collection of herbs which he supposed would have medical value.

The next day a great parade took place throughout the city streets. Columbus rode on a white horse at its head with the King on one side and the Prince on the other. Then followed the crew carrying live parrots, popinjays, small mammals and a few stuffed animals which they brought from the islands. The people were most amazed at the sight of the six painted natives, survivors of the ten with whom Columbus started on the return voyage. They were called Indians, because Columbus thought he had discovered the coast of India.

Bibliography

Samuel Eliot Morison, *Admiral of the Ocean Sea* (Boston: Little, Brown, 1942).

What Is an American?

Letter from an American Farmer—Hector St Jean de Crevecoeur
1735-1813

In this great American Asylum, the poor of Europe have by some means met together, and in consequence of various causes; to what purpose should they ask one another what countrymen are they? Alas, two-thirds of them had no country. Can a wretch, who works and starves, whose life is in a continual scene of sore affliction or pinching penury; can that man call England, or any other Kingdom, his country? A country that had no bread for him, whose fields procured him no harvest, who met with nothing but the frown of the rich, the severity of the laws, with jails and punishment; who owned not a single foot of the extensive surface of this planet? No! Urged by a variety of motives, here they came. Everything has tended to regiment them; new laws, a new mode of living, a new social system; here they are become men; in Europe they were so many useless plants, wanting vegetation mold and refreshing showers; they withered and were mowed down by want, hunger, and war; but now by the power of transplantation, like all the plants, they have taken roots and flourished! Formerly, they were not numbered on any civil list of their country, except in those of the poor; here they rank as citizens. By what invisible power has this surprising metamorphosis been performed? By that of the laws and that of their industry. The laws, the indulgent laws, protect them as they arrive, stamping upon them the symbol of adoption; they receive ample rewards for their labours; these accumulated rewards procure them lands; those lands confer on them the title of freemen, and to that title every benefit is affixed which men can possibly require. This is the great operation duty performed by our laws. From whence proceed our laws? From our government. Whence the government?

122

It is derived from the original genius and strong desire of the people. . . .

What then is the American, this new man? . . . He is an American, who leaving behind him all his ancient prejudices and manners, receives new ones from the new mode of life he has embraced, the new government he obeys, and the new rank he holds. He becomes an American by being received in the broad lap of our great Alma Mater. Here individuals of all nations are melted into a new race of men, whose labours and posterity will one day cause great changes in the world . . . The American is a new man, who acts upon new principles; he must therefore entertain new ideas, and form new opinions. From involuntary idleness, servile dependence, penury, and useless labour, he has passed to toils of a very different nature, rewarded by ample subsistence. This is an American.

11. VETERAN'S DAY—NOVEMBER 11

Our first Armistice Day was made legal by Congress, November 11, 1921. The date marked the fourth anniversary of the signing of an armistice with Germany and the day was set aside to honor the veterans of World War I. However, we have had to fight in two other foreign wars—World War II and the Korean War—so President Eisenhower signed a bill in June, 1954, that would include these soldiers as well. The name of the holiday was also changed to "Veteran's Day."

The day is usually celebrated by displaying flags everywhere and holding a parade of veterans in each community. Since the armistice with Germany was signed at 11 A.M. on November 11, 1918, it is customary to observe two minutes of silence at that hour —even on the radio. The "Great Silence" was originated by George Honey, an Australian journalist, who died in 1922. Churches throughout America observe Veteran's Day the preceding Sunday by offering patriotic services and prayers for the dead.

The most solemn service observed anywhere is the laying of a wreath on the grave of the Unknown Soldier. The ceremony takes place in the Arlington National Cemetery, and the President and other dignitaries take part. On the same day, in London, a similar ceremony takes place in Westminster Abbey, where the Unknown

Soldier was buried among English kings and queens. A maple leaf from a Canadian comrade was placed in the same grave. Paris also selected an unidentified soldier and buried him in a sarcophagus which was placed in the Arc de Triomphe. There a perpetual flame burns in honor of France's dead.

The story of how America chose her Unknown Soldier should be familiar to everyone. In France there are four American cemeteries filled with white crosses—Belleau, Bony, Romagne and Thiancourt. A body was taken from each cemetery to City Hall in Chalôns-sur-Marne and placed in a flag-draped room. While an army band played the sad notes of a funeral dirge, a sergeant of the Fifty-ninth Infantry placed a bouquet of white roses on one of the coffins. This casket was marked with the inscription:

"An Unknown American Soldier who gave his life in the Great War."

The body arrived in Washington November 9 and remained lying in state in the rotunda of the Capitol for three days. King George V sent a message in his own handwriting:

"As unknown, and yet well known, as dying, and behold, we live."

In the streets on Veteran's Day one sees little flags in the windows bearing blue or gold stars—symbols of the men in each family who fought in the wars. The blue stars are for the living and the gold tells of the son who never came home. It is the custom for veterans to sell poppies throughout the day to aid wounded veterans of all three wars. Poppies are also sold on Memorial Day. They serve as a reminder that since recorded history no war has ever ended in lasting peace. The person who buys a poppy renews a promise that he who lies dead shall not have died in vain.

In the Presbyterian Meeting churchyard in Alexandria, Virginia, there is another tomb of an Unknown Soldier—this was a soldier of the Revolution. Engraved upon it is a tribute by William Tyler Page:

Here lies the soldier of
The Revolution whose identity
Is unknown but to God.

His was an idealism
That recognized a Supreme
Being, that planted
Religious liberty on our
Shores, that overthrew
Despotism, that established
A people's government
That wrote a Constitution
Setting metes and bounds
Of delegated authority,
That fixed a standard of
Value upon men above
Gold and lifted high the
Torch of civil liberty
Along the paths of
Mankind.

In ourselves his soul
Exists as part of ours,
His memory mansion.

FROM "UNKNOWN" BY BRUCE BARTON

But the real inscription will not be written on any stone; it will stand in dictionaries of the future. Only by writing it thus can the world keep faith with the long sad procession of its unknown heroes whom it has lied to and cheated and fooled.

This will be the inscription:

War
An Armed Contest Between Nations—
Now Obsolete
Unknown

126

AMERICAN VETERANS OF SIX WARS

The display of flags on Veteran's Day is as great as that on any other patriotic holiday. This is due to the nature of most November 11 celebrations and the fact that everyone in the community takes part in the program. Most towns and cities have a parade during the day followed by patriotic speeches, either in a church or a specially erected platform. In preparation for this, large flags are flown from public buildings, store windows decorated with red, white and blue bunting, and every home that possesses a flag finds a way to display it. Therefore, since flags are the order of the day, it is important to know how to display them properly:

On a speaker's platform

If an American flag is flown from a staff, it is placed in the position of honor at the speaker's right and front.

When the flag is displayed on the wall, it should be above and behind the speaker.

The focal point of a parade is the reviewing stand, and later, the speakers' platform or gathering place for a special program. The first contingent in the line of march is usually headed by a display of many different banners other than the Stars and Stripes, but the American flag must always be included as shown in the illustration.

The United States flag is carried in front of the center of the line.

If there are several hundred people in a parade, the marchers are usually divided into small groups led by different bands. This not only distributes the music, but military and fraternal uniforms lend color and keep up interest in the parade. Each organization—such as regiments, scouts, fraternal organizations, etc.—carries an identifying banner along with the American flag, as shown in the illustration.

The United States flag is on the marching right of another flag when carried in a procession.

Some Do's and Don'ts in a Parade

1. *On Veteran's Day* all flags are flown at *full mast* along the line of march.

2. *Salute to national anthem.* When the "Star Spangled Banner" is played and the flag is not displayed, all present should stand and face toward the music. When the flag is displayed, the regular salute to the flag should be given.

3. *When flags of other nations* are carried with that of the United States, all staffs should be the same height and the flags of approximately equal size. International usage forbids the display of the flag of one nation above another nation in time of peace.

4. *On a float* in a parade the flag is displayed from a staff as shown in the illustration.

5. *On an automobile,* the flag may be fastened to the body, or clamped to the radiator cap, but always from a staff.

6. When frequency of rising and saluting a flag tends to make the act irksome or ludicrous as numerous flags in a parade go by, it is considered proper to merely remove the hat and place it at the left shoulder as each flag passes, without rising.

7. *The staff* of the flag is held in one or both hands, in front of the center of the body, the staff at an angle of about thirty degrees from the body.

8. *The Flag Code says,* "Do not dip the flag of the United States to any person or anything. The regimental color, state flag or organizational or institutional flag will render this honor." However, the Navy regulations permit the flag to be dipped on a few specified occasions.

UNIFORMS OF WOMEN IN WORLD WARS I AND II

Community celebrations in honor of patriotic holidays usually include a parade of some kind. In smaller towns everyone joins in the merrymaking, and marching to music delights both young and old. There are a number of devices one may use to make a parade an unusual event. One, of course, is colorful costumes depicting one theme or another, with streamers and balloons of various colors. "Parade lanterns" are most effective in a night parade and, in general, there are two types, as shown in the illustration.

A. Cut windows out of the sides of cardboard cartons and cover the openings with transparent paper. On each wall paste colored cutouts or motifs cut from construction paper. Two long poles are pushed through the lower part to serve as handles. Illuminate by placing some sort of flashlight in the center.

B. Another type of lantern is one that can be attached to a long pole to be carried high above the head. The walls can be cut from tin cans or cardboard.

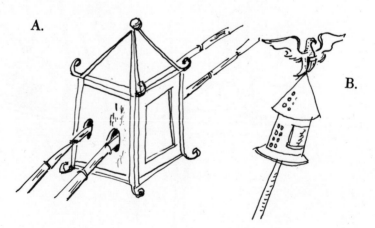

A.

B.

When the parade is over, try to end it with a special event rather than let it fizzle out. One way is to form a human flag and another, to have a drill of some kind. On the following pages you will find a few special drill figures.

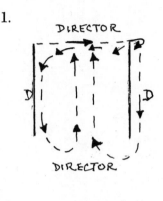

1.

Diagrams of Some Drill Figures

1. *Circle Counter March.* Participants form two lines at opposite ends of the field. The ones in the north lines march south, turn east and then north. The others, in the south line march north, turn east and then south, passing on the inside of the other line. When the leaders meet, move up center of field to west.

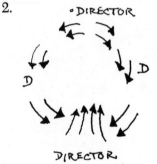

2.

2. *Fours.* The first two in line turn to the right and the next two to the left. Continue around the field to the east and up in fours.

3. *Cross.* Again the first two in line turn to right and the next two to left. One member of each group steps behind his partner making a single line. When leaders reach the corners, turn to opposite corner of the field. Then turn to center and up in twos.

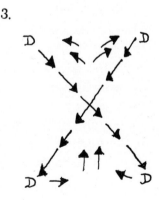

3.

133

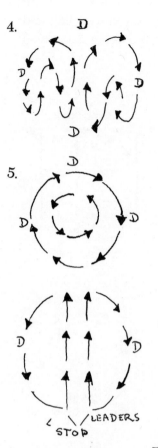

4. *Snake Trail.* One to the right and one to the left. March down outside of the field, then follow diagram.

5. *Opposite Circles.* One to the right, one to the left. Line turning to the right form outside circle. Line turning to the left form inside line. The two circles march in opposite directions. When whistle blows to stop, continue marching until the leaders meet. Up in twos ready for next formation.

6. *Snail.* One to the right, one to the left. When leaders meet at opposite end of field, the leaders stop, participants form circle. One leader winds inside circle as per diagram. When snail is wound, all face opposite direction. Leader at end of snail leads everyone out.*

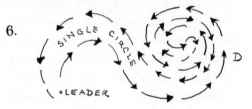

Forming a Human Flag

A large human flag can be formed by children or adults dressed in red, white and blue. The dimensions and positions of the stripes, stars and blue field should be carefully marked on the surface where the flag is to be formed. (See page 72 for dimensions of flag—which, however, are frequently modified in the forming of human flags.)

It requires at least four hundred persons, 50 in white representing the stars; 96 in blue, the blue field; 136 in red, the red stripes; 120 in white, the white stripes.

* Taken from Department of Public Recreation, Decatur, Ill.

The costumes can be made of crepe paper or inexpensive cloth. If the participants kneel to form the flag, it is possible to wear red, white and blue capes instead of a full dress in these colors. The cape is pulled up over the head when they are in the proper formation.

Our Flag

by Henry Ward Beecher

Our flag means all that our fathers meant in the Revolutionary War.

It means all that the Declaration of Independence meant.

It means justice.

It means liberty.

It means happiness.

Our flag carries American ideas, American history, and American feelings.

Every color means liberty.

Every thread means liberty.

Every star and stripe means liberty.

It does not mean lawlessness, but liberty through the law, and laws for liberty.

Forget not what it means.

And for the sake of its ideas, be true to your country's flag.

12. VIGNETTES OF AMERICAN PATRIOTS

Singing Tableaux

This technique was used in early Greek theaters where there were no curtains used to indicate scenes and acts in a play. On one side of the stage was a group of singers (the Greeks used women) and their songs were used to create a mood for the act that was to come. If the story was to be dramatized as a tableau or in pantomime, the music continued; otherwise, the singing stopped and the characters spoke.

America has many patriots who helped to make this a great country, so we decided to select some interesting vignettes of their lives and suggest they be used for this type of production. The libraries are full of stories about Benjamin Franklin, Henry Clay, Patrick Henry, etc., and it is easy to find songs that will fit the period.

If you have a chorus of fine singers in your community, make it an evening of patriotic songs and add tableaux as variety. On the other hand, if it is a drama group you wish to feature, have the chorus sing an appropriate song to introduce the tableau, and then have the characters speak or act their parts.

Benjamin Franklin

Benjamin Franklin gave America a sense of national unity when it needed it most, and helped America to attain independence. He was a scholar, inventor, statesman, and perhaps the world will remember him most for his greatest literary work—*Poor Richard's Almanac*. It included thoughts and axioms gleaned from everywhere and pleased Americans of all classes.

One of his greatest achievements, and one not often mentioned, was that he became the first Postmaster General of this country.

The Continental Congress appointed Dr. Franklin Postmaster General in 1775. Shortly thereafter he sent a letter of instructions to the postmasters of all the colonies. This letter was illustrated with a woodcut showing a post rider on horseback. It became a symbol for the United States Post Office and is still used today. It appeared on early postage stamps, seals, documents, and was even used for the manufacture of Post Office Department buttons.

John Adams

John Adams, our second President, was inaugurated on March 4, 1797. He was the first Chief Executive to reside in the White House in Washington, having previously lived at various places, including the Union Tavern in Georgetown. Eyewitnesses say he left the Tavern reluctantly; waving a tankard of ale to his friend, he coined that timeless remark: "I shall return."

137

Lafayette

"Fortunate, Fortunate man!
Heaven saw fit to order that the
electric spark of liberty should be
conducted, through Lafayette,
from the Old World to the New."
—Daniel Webster

Lafayette, the young French nobleman who gave up his pleasurable life at court to help us fight for freedom, is one of America's most beloved patriots. He was eighteen years old when he informed his uncle of his desire to go to America and help win the Revolution.

Count Broglie replied:

"I have seen your uncle die in the wars in Italy. I witnessed your father's death at the Battle of Munden, and I will not be accessory to the ruin of the only remaining branch of the family."

Lafayette said:

"My zeal and love of liberty have perhaps been hitherto the prevailing motives; but now I see a chance for usefulness which I had not anticipated. I have money; I will purchase a ship, which shall convey to America myself, my companions, and the freight for Congress."

Upon his arrival in America, Lafayette asked for two favors only—first, "to serve at my own expense"; second, "to commence serving as a volunteer." But Congress commissioned him a major general at once, and he became one of Washington's most trusted officers and friends. The friendship between Washington and Lafayette is one of the beautiful ones recorded in history.

President Monroe said:

"You are ours by the unmistakable gratitude for your services which is a precious portion of our inheritance; ours by that tie of love, stronger than death, which has linked your name for the endless ages of time with the name of Washington."

Lafayette said:

"I have come many miles to see the 'Young General!' . . . I have

138

had two happy days in my life—one, when I landed with you on the American coast nearly fifty years ago, and today when I see your face again. I have lived long enough."

Of Lafayette's three children, two received American names. His only son was named George Washington and one of his daughters was named Virginia. While Lafayette, his wife and two daughters were in the Olmutz Prison, his son, then seventeen, managed to escape to America. Washington arranged for him to enter Harvard in 1795 and gave him permission to draw on him any amount of money.

Lafayette loved America too. He wrote a letter to his wife: "I am now in the city [Philadelphia], where everyone is much after the English fashion, except that there are more simplicity, equality, cordiality, and courtesy here than in England. The American women are very pretty, simple in their manners, and exhibit a neatness which is everywhere cultivated. What most charms me is, that all the citizens are brethren. In America, there are no poor, nor even what we call peasantry. Each individual has his own honest property and the same rights as the most wealthy proprietor."

And America loved Lafayette. When Lafayette died in 1834, the state of Virginia shipped Virginia earth to France, that he might be buried in American soil. And at the head of the grave is an American flag and there have been flowers put there continuously since his death. Count René Chanbrun, his great, great, greatgrandson, wrote after the Second World War: "During the long, dark years of German occupation, it may well have been the only American flag in occupied Europe, a secret spot of hope."

Washington's Farewell to His Officers
(as told by Washington Irving)

In a course of a few days Washington prepared to depart for Annapolis, where Congress was assembling, with the intention of asking leave to resign his command. A barge was in waiting about noon on the fourth of December at Whitehall ferry to convey him across the Hudson to Paulus Hook. The principal officers of the

139

army assembled at Fraunces' Tavern in the neighborhood of the ferry, to take a final leave of him. On entering the room, and finding himself surrounded by his old companions in arms, who had shared with him so many scenes of hardship, difficulty and danger, his agitated feelings overcame his usual self-command. Filling a glass of wine, and turning upon them his benignant but saddened countenance, "With a heart full of love and gratitude," said he, "I now take leave of you, most devoutly wishing that your latter days may be prosperous and happy as your former ones have been glorious and honorable."

Having drunk his farewell benediction, he added with emotion, "I cannot come to each of you to take my leave, but shall be obliged if each of you will come and take me by the hand."

General Knox, who was the nearest, was the first to advance. Washington, affected even to tears, grasped his hand and gave him a brother's embrace. In the same affectionate manner he took leave of the rest. Not a word was spoken. The deep feeling and manly tenderness of these veterans in the parting moment could find no utterance in words. Silent and solemn they followed their loved commander as he left the room, passed through a corps of light infantry, and proceed on foot to Whitehall ferry. Having entered the barge, he turned to them, took off his hat and waved a silent adieu. They replied in the same manner, and having watched the barge until the intervening point of the Battery shut it from sight, returned, still solemn and silent, to the place where they had assembled.

Thomas Jefferson

"The tree of liberty must be refreshed from time
to time with the blood of patriots and tyrants."

Thomas Jefferson, third President of the United States, was the author of the Declaration of Independence and founder of the Republican party. He was a philosopher who believed:

1. There was good in all men.
2. To make America prosperous, there should be a wise and

140

frugal government which would restrain men from injuring one another and leave them otherwise to regulate their own pursuits of industry and improvement and not take from the mouth of labor the bread it has earned.

3. There should be less government spending, fewer taxes, less army and navy, less social snobbery and no entangling alliances with other countries.

4. There should be more libraries, schools, newspapers, more American land reclaimed by farmers and more imported seeds to plant.

5. Most important, the Republican party was founded by Thomas Jefferson in answer to the basic question which divided the first Cabinet:

"Can the average run of mankind govern themselves?" as Jefferson thought; or must they be governed by a privileged class of the rich, the well-born, and the good, as the Federalists believed?

6. A little rebellion now and then is as necessary in the political world as storms are in the physical world.

Jefferson designed a plow and invented the swivel chair, played the violin, introduced broom corn in Virginia and was a gifted architect, among other accomplishments.

Alexander Hamilton

"Take care of that pistol; it is un-
discharged, and still cocked. Pendleton
knows that I did not intend to fire it."

A week before their dual, Aaron Burr and Alexander Hamilton met at the annual banquet of the Society of Cincinnati, of which Hamilton was president and Burr a member. It is related that Hamilton was cheery and sometimes merry during the evening. As the feast wore away, he was urged to sing the only song he was ever known to sing—"The Drum," a famous old Scottish ballad. At first he was reluctant but finally said: "Well, you shall have it."

141

THE DRUM

Hear the gentle sheep soft bleat
    Ba-a-ah, ba-a-ah
As the wheel like soldier's feet
    Ra-ta-tah, ra-ta-tah
Like their gentle souls we came
    Ba-a-ah, ba-a-ah
And the sheepskin makes our drum
    Ra-ta-tah!
    Ra-ta-tah!
    Ra-ta-tah!

Hear the lover sigh
For his love he'll march and die
Helpless hands to overcome
Like the fingers on the drum.

Hear the little children weep
Like the tender little sheep
But their terrors rouse the dumb
And their sob is in the drum.

Do you see this harmless flock?
Filing up the mountain rock
There is nothing quarrelsome
In the bleating of our drum

We are only clad in wool
We are marching in from school
And the lesson that we hum
You shall hear upon the drum.

If the wolf is in these hills
'Tis the fife the wolf that thrills
'Tis a little drummer's thumb
Thrills the sheepskin to the drum.

Can that be Columbia's cry
Forward march! For she may die
Dear Mother, straight we come
'Tis your sons with fife and drum.

While Hamilton's song "The Drum" was sung to rollicking music, the words have a plaintive meaning. It is true that the drum can be considered a patriotic symbol, as well as an instrument of war. There are three kinds of military drums: the snare drum of the infantry, the bass drum and the brass or copper kettledrum used by the cavalry.

The drum is one of the four instruments used in the military band for field music; the fife, trumpet and bugle are the other three. Aside from their use in marching, to beat time, drums were also used for signals. We associate the Civil War with drums and with the drummer boys, who are known to have joined the colors at ages as early as twelve years. During the battle, they took their station near the commander in order to be at hand for orders to signal retreat, charge or assembly.

143

Robert E. Lee

"When the war was over The North
had Victory. The South had Lee."

Robert E. Lee was an inner man, not an outer man—he never wrote books or made speeches. The southerners admired his humility and earnestness in peace as well as his audacity in war. At Lee's surrender at Appomattox, John S. Wise said:

"You are the country to these men. They have fought for you without pay, or clothes, or care of any sort; their devotion to you and faith in you have been the only things which have held this army together."

Lee truly loved his horse, Traveler, who carried him through most of the fighting during the war. He once wrote a description of him to a friend, Martha (Martie) Williams:

"If I were an artist, I would draw a true picture of Traveler; representing his. fine proportions, muscular figure, deep chest, short back, strong haunches, flat legs, small head, broad forehead, delicate ears, quick eye, small feet and black mane and tail. Such a picture would inspire a poet, whose genius could then depict his worth and describe his endurance of toil, hunger, thirst, heat and cold, and the dangers and sufferings through which he passed. He could dilate upon his sagacity and affection, and his invariable response to every wish of his rider. He might even imagine his thoughts through the long night-marches and the days of battle through which he has passed. But I am no artist, Martie, and can therefore only say he is a Confederate Gray."

13. PATRIOTIC COLLECTIONS

Making a collection of some kind is a wonderful hobby that can be pursued either by individuals or groups. It is the kind of activity that can be laid aside on extremely active days, but it always there to provide entertainment for passive hours at a moment's notice. In order to attain the utmost joy from a collection, you should keep a scrapbook of clippings, learn something about the history of your subject, and most important of all, label each item and display it in a professional manner.

If you want to direct your collection toward education, it can be accomplished in many ways: by reading books, frequenting hobby shops where one is allowed to browse around or examining collections in libraries and museums. At the beginning you will probably start a general collection, but later on it is more practical to limit yourself to one field that has a definite beginning and end. This certainly will pose no problem because there are so many categories from which to choose.

Of course, in this book, we are interested in items that have a patriotic connotation or historical significance. Four of the nation's most popular hobbies—collecting glass, coins, buttons and stamps—are most suitable because the items are usually inexpensive and can be found without going far afield. When it comes to value the subject is open, because much depends on the law of supply and demand, and what seems unimportant today may be sought after tomorrow.

If you are looking for patriotic items, an old bottle is usually most rewarding. Since they were usually made to cast aside, the manufacturers did not bother to remove impurities from the glass, thus leaving an interesting wall full of bubbles, bits of sand and even vegetation. The color and shapes of the bottles have a primitive charm that manufacturers do not try to imitate today. The peculiar tints are due to careless mixtures of mineral dyes in the glass, and their odd crooked walls were never straightened.

Searching for an old bottle can be great fun—people left them in so many unseen places years ago. You might look in corners of attics and cellars, under boards in torn-down rooms, under porch floors or even buried deep in the ground. The next step is to clean the bottles so the glass will sparkle in the sunlight. If they are in bad condition, soak them overnight in water and then try to remove the dirt from the inside by using a long-handled brush. Add some Clorox to the water if there is mildew or mold. Finally, wash in warm soapy water and put some ammonia in the rinse water.

The bottles illustrated on page 147 showing patriotic decorations were selected at random. Note the motifs are eagles, heads of Presidents—and one is in the shape of a log cabin. It used to be the custom of political parties to distribute bottles filled with "spirits" to potential voters during a presidential campaign. The design on these bottles either carried a picture of the candidate, or there was some sort of a slogan. A complete set of campaign bottles would, indeed, be a prize for any collector.

Patriotic Decorations on Glass

The manufacture of glass was one of the first important industries in America because its basic raw material—sand—was found in abundance. The factories followed the river beds westward to Pittsburgh and along the Ohio River. The young country pulsed with patriotism, so the popular decorations were designs that either depicted a historical event or bore a patriotic title such as

   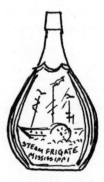

GLASS BOTTLES

Continental, Westward Ho, or Log Cabin.

After a man named Robinson invented a machine, in 1827, that would "press" glass into a mold, it was manufactured in such abundance one could never envision a shortage! However, glass is easily broken and today collectors are busy finding odd pieces to complete matching sets. Several American glass companies are reproducing old patterns, which annoys the antiquarian but pleases the person who wishes to purchase a set of goblets, or other items, simply for their beauty in form and design.

In general, two types of glass were manufactured during the eighteenth century—clear (sometimes in color), and opaque, called milk glass. Some of the items in each category come in the same shapes and have the same decorations if they were made by the same manufacturers. All the companies issued commemorative plates such as the one shown of George Washington. Other well-known plates are:

1. Head of President Garfield. Also, a second upon his assassination with the words, "We mourn our Nation's Loss."

2. Grant's peace plate with the inscription "Let us have Peace."

3. Cleveland and Hendricks campaign plate.

4. Liberty Bell—100 years.

5. Heroes of Bunker Hill 1776-1876 with names Prescott and Putnam.

Most of the items were made in milk glass during the Spanish American War. The most popular are covered dishes bearing the American eagle, Admiral Dewey, Uncle Sam, the battleship *Maine*, Dewey's flagship, etc.

Collecting United States Coins

Collecting United States coins is an inexpensive hobby that may be indulged in by almost anyone. One thing is certain—the value of each coin in your collection has a chance to go up but never down. If you want to pursue this fascinating hobby, first purchase some special folders sold at most hobby shops and ten-cent stores that will accommodate various dimensions of United States coins. Second, secure a book that will tell the history of the

MILK GLASS DISHES

various coins and something about their value. Here are a few hints:

> Rarest Coin—gold piece, minted 1849—one only minted
> Most valuable dollar—1804—only a few minted
> Most valuable quarter—1823 (very rare)
> Most valuable dime—1894 with the "S" mint mark
> Most valuable Indian Head cent—1877
> Most valuable Lincoln penny—1909 with mint mark "S"
>   and underneath initials V D B

The value of a coin depends on the number minted and put into circulation that year. Everyone looks for a 1913 Liberty Head nickel, but such a coin is a myth because it never existed. The design of the nickel was changed to the Buffalo type that year and only six "unauthorized" nickels were struck that year by employees at the mint. All six are now in private collections.

DIFFERENT CATEGORIES FOR COLLECTIONS

1. Obsolete types and denominations—United States half cent, large cent, half dime, two-cent, three-cent and twenty-cent pieces.
2. Acquire different dates in best possible condition.
3. Collect coins only dated year of your birth.
4. Scarce coins obtained from dealers.

Bibliography

Wilfred Dellguest, *United States Coins—A Guide to Values* (New York: M. Barrows, 1951.)
Hobby Magazine.

Collecting Patriotic Buttons

A button collector who wishes to collect only ones with patriotic insignia has a fertile field indeed. One may spend a lifetime collecting military buttons alone, as this subject is unlimited, no matter where you live. Consider the millions of buttons worn by veterans of six wars, plus ones worn by soldiers in time of peace,

150

UNITED STATES COINS

PATRIOTIC BUTTONS

such as the G.A.R. Even so, many styles ignored today may well be sought for as a rarity in another fifty years. Tens of thousands of military buttons have gone into eternity with the uniformed remains of interred veterans and as many thrown away by uninterested persons. Anyone interested in this category will find excellent help in David Johnson's book on *Military Buttons*. It is not often a collector can locate material on one category so well defined and classified.

Patriotic designs on buttons often run parallel to ones found on stamps. It is always interesting to find a decoration on a button that is familiar from having seen a stamp, or vice versa. Sometimes the designs are identical, but more often it has a different rendering of the same subject; particularly buttons that depict memorable scenes in American history. If you are interested in making such a parallel collection, here are a few hints:

> Great seal of the United States
> Portraits of Presidents and American patriots
> Liberty Bell
> Landing of Columbus
> Pony Express and Franklin's Post Riders
> Seals of different states

Another subject ever popular on old buttons is portraits and heads of American patriots. These include, for instance, George Washington, Christopher Columbus, Henry Clay, Lafayette, Abraham Lincoln and many others. Buttons depicting scenes in our country's history are most sought after—they are usually made of metal and the decorations show fine craftsmanship in their engravings and design.

Confederate Buttons were imported from New England and Europe so are identified mostly by insignia. The usual decoration was an eagle surrounded by seven or nine stars.

Grand Army Buttons usually carried a G.A.R. monogram.

Washington and Lafayette Buttons

It is not known at present who made the George Washington buttons, but it is generally believed that they were made by English button makers who used Washington's popularity to further their button business. They are slightly convex, 34 millimeters in diameter and made of metal which was shaped in a mold.

When the Marquis de Lafayette visited this country in 1824, the Scovill Button Company of Texas presented to him a set of buttons "as a token of appreciation of his war service to this country." These buttons, seventeen in number, were made from solid gold and featured a head of George Washington. The gold was obtained from a single nugget unearthed in North Carolina. "Magnifique!" exclaimed Lafayette.

Collecting United States Stamps

Stamp collecting, no doubt, stands at the top of the list of favorite hobbies enjoyed by American people today. It is an ever-

UNITED STATES FLAGS

154

present one that can be enjoyed over a lifetime, because each year new and beautiful stamps are issued to be added to a collection. Stamp collecting is not only fun, it is educational as well. It is a leisure-time activity that appeals to all age groups and classes of people, and it can be as interesting as you desire to make it.

United States stamps reflect our nation's history and growth almost from the very beginning. In fact, they might be regarded as an official record of our memorable events. A stamp is not just a piece of paper which laws require one to purchase in order to mail a letter or send a package. Every stamp issued carries its own little story. Every one is of interest and value if it is properly understood and taken care of, so let's see how a beginner can get started:

AMERICAN ARTISTS

Plate Block. When a stamp collector speaks of a plate block, he is referring to the four corner stamps which have the plate number (on the outer edge) attached to the block of stamps. On a sheet of stamps one may find dots, lines, engravings of all sorts, and the center lines which divide it into four sections. They are usually there so that the post office clerk can easily see where to tear off twenty-five from the sheet, or any number of stamps desired, without counting out every stamp.

155

Watermarks. Underneath the gum on the back of many stamps are watermarks of the paper on which they are printed. Stamp collectors often want to examine watermarks in order to determine the authenticity of stamps. If a watermark cannot be seen with the naked eye, add some benzine, which will not destroy the stamp or color but will remove the glue. . . . United States stamps have what are called single-line and double-line watermarks—that is, the letters of the watermarks are of single and double lines.

AMERICAN POETS

There are so many interesting bypaths down which a collector may wander, it might be well to try several before choosing a subject or category. First of all, it is important to buy a stamp catalogue to help in identifying stamps and learning about their value. Next, an album is essential if stamps are to be kept in good condition. There are many types on the market. A looseleaf type of album is the most practical because it allows for continuous expansion without transferring and rehandling of stamps.

Since we are concerned only with United States stamps in this chapter, let us tell you a few basic facts about how stamps are printed and marketed:

Coils are not issued in sheets but in rolls, and are found in stamp machines. They have straight edges on two sides, either vertical or horizontal.

Booklets have six stamps on a page and are called "panes." To the collector, stamps such as these are more interesting; they must be in a pane of six to prove their origin.

Building a Special Collection

What special collections are possible? They are limited only by your ingenuity and the extent to which you wish to pursue stamp collecting. Specialization means hunting, searching and observing, but this should be a constant source of pleasure, possessing all the qualities of other recreational pursuits. You will become more conscious of stamp designs and come to appreciate the artistic qualities of stamps as well as their physical characteristics and markings.

PRESIDENTS OF THE U.S.

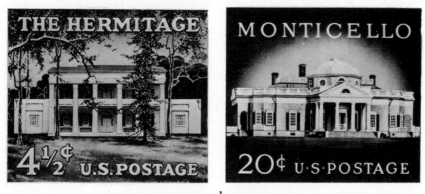

PRESIDENTS' HOMES

STATEHOOD STAMPS

New postage series, in the United States, are changed roughly every fifteen years. In 1938 the entire postage set portrayed every President of the United States from Washington through Harding (by law living persons, including Presidents, may not be portrayed on a stamp).

A new series was started in 1954 and the subjects were divided so that six stamps were devoted to great Presidents, six to other famous Americans and six to historic shrines.

The so-called "Liberty" series was so planned that it was non-political (including Thomas Jefferson, Woodrow Wilson, Abraham Lincoln and Theodore Roosevelt). All of these stamps are basically the same size as the first stamp, which was issued in 1840.

Where commemoratives or semipostals are concerned "occasion" becomes a major factor. The United States Post Office Department feels that twelve to fifteen commemorative stamps a year are enough. It is therefore necessary for postal authorities to screen carefully the many requests and pick those of greatest national importance. The special Astronaut stamp was issued the day Lieutenant Colonel John Glenn made his three orbits around the earth and this was the first time in history a commemorative stamp was issued on the day the event happened.

The stamps shown in the illustration are part of the American "Credo" series issued in 1960. They express beliefs propounded by prominent Americans such as George Washington, Benjamin Franklin, Thomas Jefferson, Patrick Henry, Francis Scott Key and Abraham Lincoln. These stamps were designed only after roughly one hundred outstanding men and women were invited to select those statements they believed most important in light of present events.

Anniversaries of statehood have been so generally honored that future events must necessarily be so honored. The newest statehood stamps celebrate the admission of Alaska and Hawaii. Historical events, particularly those that happened exactly three hundred, two hundred or one hundred years ago, are seriously considered each year.

Thus, one can see a stamp collector can be busy just keeping pace with the new yearly issues. Besides the commemoratives and regular issues, the United States government for many years has made stamps for outlying territories—Puerto Rico, the Canal Zone, etc. So you see, collecting United States stamps can be a "world without end."

AMERICAN CREDO ISSUE

14. PATRIOTIC GAMES AND SONGS FOR CHILDREN

Here are a few children's games on a patriotic theme that may be played at any American celebration. No effort has been made to develop a large number, because any game can become a patriotic one by the simple expedient of giving it a new name which has a patriotic connotation. Every leader usually has a store of favorite games for his children, and when a patriotic holiday comes along, he doesn't shelve all in favor of a complete stock of new ones. For example, teams can be called the reds, whites and blues; you can have a relay between the Minute Men and the British, and for a quiet game, fill George Washington's trunk. However, here are a few games you may not have thought of.

The Waving Flags

The children are divided into two equal teams. The first child in each team has a flag. He must move in and out between each member of his team down to the end of the line and then back to his original position, continuously waving the flag. As the flag waves, the children chant, "We are Americans." Once the child with the flag has returned to his place, he passes it to the next child who in turn moves in and out, back and forth, between the children. The team wins the game which first has every child carry the flag.

Drawing the Flag

It is a wise child that knows all about the United States flag—here is a game based on this idea. A flag presents an easy problem for a child to draw, so give each one a large piece of white construction paper and a red and blue crayon. When they get to work, tell them it matters not whether they know how to do it correctly as long as they are willing to learn. Here are some of the points to emphasize (see pages 71-72).

1. The seven red stripes and six white ones.
2. The red stripes being on the outside of the flag.
3. Where to place the blue canton in relation to the stripes.
4. How many rows of stars and the number in each row.
5. One point of the star always being on top.

The Old Soldier

Players are seated in a circle. One child walks around holding a pen, a pencil or a picture which indicates "an old soldier." He holds it up and asks one of the children, "What will you give the old soldier?" The child asked must not use the words *red, white, blue, yes* or *no* in his answer. If he does, he must pay a forfeit.

Example:

"What will you give the old soldier—a Purple Heart?"
"Oh, you can't do that—only the President can give a Purple Heart."
"Will you give him a coat?"
"I do not think I will." (Avoid saying *no*).
"What will you give him then—a hat?"
"Well, I think I will."

Only three questions are asked of each player. If one breaks the rules, he must pay a forfeit. The leader must ask all the questions.

You can adapt this game to a particular holiday, substituting Lincoln or Washington, for example, for the Old Soldier. The

leader should be familiar with their backgrounds in order to vary the questions.

Children love to march to the rhythm of a drum. It is not necessary for the children to be dressed as soldiers but it will add zest to a game if they wear a soldier's hat or carry a flag. The drummer definitely should be dressed in costume. He should be an older boy who not only knows how to play a drum, but can lead a line of march.

Here are some marching games for young children with simple figures they can follow:

"Ten Small Soldiers"

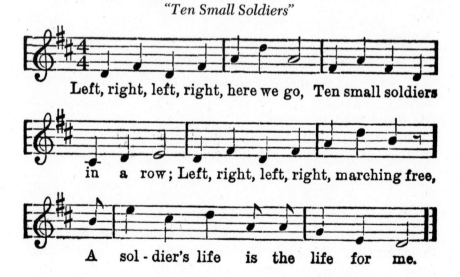

Left, right, left, right, here we go, Ten small soldiers in a row; Left, right, left, right, marching free, A sol-dier's life is the life for me.

"Soldier-Boy, Soldier-Boy"

Sol-dier-boy, Sol-dier-boy, where are you go - ing,

Bear- ing so proud -ly the red, white and blue? I'm

go -ing where country and du - ty are call-ing, If

you'll be a sol - dier-boy you may go too.

Divide the children into two groups (it is not necessary to have boys in one and girls in the other, unless there is an even number of each). Have them stand in two lines on opposite sides of the room. The first line will sing "Soldier-boy," etc., and the other line answers, "I'm going," etc. As they sing "You may go too," the soldier line advances across the room and the children salute each other when they meet. They then join hands and march in double formation around the room. Each team takes its position on the opposite side of the room, and the second team becomes the soldiers.

163

WITH TRUMPET AND DRUM.

Poem by EUGENE FIELD.

Music by CARO S. SENOUR.

1. With big ___ tin trum-pet and lit - tle red drum, Marching like sold - iers the child - ren come! It's this way and that way they cir - cle and file, My! but that mu - sic of

2. Come on, lit - tle peo - ple, from cot and from hall, This heart it hath wel - come and room for you all! It will sing you its songs and warm you with love, As your dear lit - tle arms with my

3. So come; though I see not his dear lit - tle face, And hear not his voice in this ju - bi - lant place, I know he were hap - py to bid me en - shrine His mem - o - ry deep in my

164

theirs   is   fine!   This way and that way and   af - ter   a   while They
arms in - ter - twine It will   rock   you   a - way   to   the   dream-land a - bove Oh a
heart with your play, Ah   me! but a love that is   sweet-er than mine

march straight in - to this heart   of ' mine! A stur - dy   old heart but   it
jol - ly old heart is this old heart of   mine; And jol - li - er still it   is
hold-eth my   boy in its keep -ing   to - day! And my heart it   is   lone - ly   so,

has to suc-cumb To   the blare of   that   trum-pet, and beat of   that drum!
bound to be-come When you blow that   big   trum-pet, and beat   that   red drum!
lit - tle folks, come, March in and make   mer - ry   with   trum - pet   and drum!

165

Minute Men's March

Young children will love playing this game. The players line up at one end of the room, and the drummer is at the other end facing the wall, or with his back to the children. The object of the game is for the players to reach the other wall without breaking the rules of the game. At the starting signal, the drummer beats the drum and the children begin to march toward the goal. They may move only when the drummer's back is turned, and he may spin around and catch them moving at any time. Anyone who is detected in the slightest movement is sent back to the starting line. The game continues with the drummer alternately facing and turning his back to the players at irregular intervals until one player has reached the wall, or goal.

Story Theater

A story theater can be carefully constructed to be used as a permanent dramatic property, or it can be made for the moment, out of cardboard and paper. Either way, the principle is the same: the theater is simply a stage furnished with a setting for a story. This includes, of course, a curtain and, if you can manage it, some sort of lighting. A permanent set might have a scene of trees and shrubs, as many of the fairy tales and nursery rhymes take place in a forest. The scenery is stationary but the characters are moved from place to place as the story unfolds.

On the bottom of the stage are numerous slits cut in numerous directions so the characters (cut in two dimensions like paper dolls) can be pushed up through from underneath and moved around the maze. The figures can be mounted at the top of a

tongue depressor and the bottom part used as a handle. The theater is set up high enough to allow a child to sit underneath to work the puppet characters.

You can also use this theater simply as a storytelling set with no action. The illustration above depicts the story of George Washington and the cherry tree.

Who Said These Immortal Words?

1. "By uniting we stand. By dividing we fall."
2. "Taxation without representation is tyranny."
3. "These are the times that try men's souls."
4. "To the memory of the man who was first in war, first in peace and first in the hearts of his countrymen."
5. "To the victor belongs the spoils."
6. "The four Freedoms termed essential—freedom of speech and expression, freedom of worship, freedom from want and freedom from fear."
7. "Posterity will talk of Washington with reverence, as the founder of a great empire, when my name shall be lost in the vortex of revolution."
8. "Millions for defense but not one cent for tribute."
9. "In bestowing charity, the main thought is to help those who help themselves."
10. "The greatest service that can be rendered to any country is to add a useful plant to its culture."
11. "I've not yet begun to fight."
12. "Dear friends and gentle hearts."
13. "A sharp tongue is the only edge tool that becomes sharper with constant use."
14. "One man with courage makes a majority."
15. "If you don't say anything, you won't be called on to repeat it."
16. "Don't hit at all if it is honorably possible to avoid hitting; but never hit soft."

For answers see page 178.

15. FACTS ABOUT THE STATES

Each state in the Union made its own individual contribution toward making our's a great nation. In fact, the criteria used for admitting a new state into the Union are to establish that the lands have been cleared and under cultivation, a responsible government exists, a system of education is in force, etc. To celebrate these events, many states have their own holidays and each has its individual seal, emblems and symbols.

Anyone looking for dramatic material will find a great source by delving into the histories of the different states—the motion picture companies have been doing this for years (for example, in Western movies). In this chapter we list many pertinent facts, but you can find others in the *World Almanac* and the public library. George Early S. Shankle's book, *State Names, Flags, Seals, Songs, Birds, Flowers, and Other Symbols* (New York: H. W. Wilson), is most helpful. It also gives a brief history of each state.

Each star in the flag of the United States represents a state; the stripes stand for the thirteen original colonies. President Taft apportioned the stars and stripes by executive order on October 26, 1912, according to the chronology in which the states ratified the Constitution or entered the Union. The diagram below indicates the apportionment of the stars by number and the names of states are printed on the stripes.

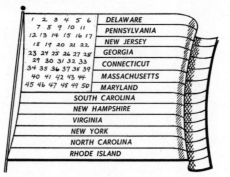

168

Apportionment of Stars by Numbers

1. Delaware—December 7, 1787
2. Pennsylvania—December 12, 1787
3. New Jersey—December 18, 1787
4. Georgia—January 2, 1788
5. Connecticut—January 9, 1788
6. Massachusetts—February 6, 1788
7. Maryland—April 28, 1788
8. South Carolina—May 23, 1788
9. New Hampshire—June 21, 1788
10. Virginia—June 25, 1788
11. New York—July 26, 1788
12. North Carolina—November 21, 1789
13. Rhode Island—May 29, 1790
14. Vermont—March 4, 1791
15. Kentucky—June 1, 1792
16. Tennessee—June 1, 1796
17. Ohio—March 1, 1803
18. Louisiana—April 30, 1812
19. Indiana—December 11, 1816
20. Mississippi—December 10, 1817
21. Illinois—December 3, 1818
22. Alabama—December 14, 1819
23. Maine—March 15, 1820
24. Missouri—August 10, 1821
25. Arkansas—June 15, 1836
26. Michigan—January 26, 1837
27. Florida—March 3, 1845
28. Texas—December 29, 1845
29. Iowa—December 28, 1846
30. Wisconsin—May 29, 1848
31. California—September 9, 1850
32. Minnesota—May 11, 1858
33. Oregon—February 14, 1859
34. Kansas—January 29, 1861
35. West Virginia—June 19, 1863
36. Nevada—October 31, 1864
37. Nebraska—March 1, 1867
38. Colorado—August 1, 1876
39. North Dakota—November 2, 1889
40. South Dakota—November 2, 1889
41. Montana—November 8, 1889
42. Washington—November 11, 1889
43. Idaho—July 3, 1890
44. Wyoming—July 10, 1890
45. Utah—January 4, 1896
46. Oklahoma—November 16, 1907
47. New Mexico—January 6, 1912
48. Arizona—February 14, 1912
49. Alaska—January 3, 1959
50. Hawaii—August 21, 1959

INDIANA

IOWA

LOUISIANA

MISSISSIPPI

MONTANA

KANSAS

KENTUCKY

MARYLAND

MINNESOTA

MAINE

MICHIGAN

MISSOURI

MASSACHUSETTS

State Seals

Seals were old when America was young, so it was only natural that the colonies and then the states were quick to adopt them officially. A seal is the closely guarded property of administrative authority, public or private, the world over. Only by its application can important documents become legally effective.

Maybe you do not realize that we start life with a seal on our birth certificate—and when we die there's a seal on our death certificate. Between these two dates we are beset with all kinds of seals—our marriage license, dog license, automobile and driver's licenses, most of our legal papers. The design of the seal will usually be that of the state in which you are residing, so look it up on the preceding pages and become familiar with it.

State	Flower	Bird	Tree
Alabama	Camellia	Yellowhammer	Southern pine
Alaska	Forget-me-not	Willow ptarmigan	(None)
Arizona	Giant cactus	Cactus wren	Paloverde
Arkansas	Apple blososm	Mockingbird	Pine
California	Golden poppy	Valley quail	Redwood
Colorado	Columbine	Lark bunting	Blue spruce
Connecticut	Mountain laurel	American robin	White oak
Delaware	Peach blossom	Blue hen chicken	American holly
Florida	Orange blossom	Mockingbird	Cabbage palmetto
Georgia	Cherokee rose	Brown thrasher	Live oak
Hawaii	Hibiscus	Nene	Coconut
Idaho	Syringa	Mountain bluebird	White pine
Illinois	Butterfly violet	Cardinal	Bur oak
Indiana	Peony	Cardinal	Tulip
Iowa	Wild prairie rose	Goldfinch	Oak
Kansas	Sunflower	Western meadow lark	Cottonwood
Kentucky	Goldenrod	Cardinal	Tulip
Louisiana	Magnolia	Brown pelican	(None)
Maine	Pine cone and tassel	Chickadee	Eastern white pine
Maryland	Black-eyed susan	Oriole	White oak
Massachusetts	Mayflower	Chickadee	American elm
Michigan	Apple blossom	Robin	White pine
Minnesota	Moccasin flower	Loon	Red pine
Mississippi	Magnolia	Mockingbird	Magnolia
Missouri	Hawthorn	Eastern bluebird	Dogwood
Montana	Bitterroot	Western meadow lark	Ponderosa pine
Nebraska	Goldenrod	Western meadow lark	Elm
Nevada	Sagebrush	Mountain bluebird	Single-leaf piñon
New Hampshire	Purple lilac	Purple finch	Paper birch
New Jersey	Purple violet	Eastern goldfinch	Red oak
New Mexico	Yucca	Road runner	Piñon
New York	Rose	Eastern bluebird	Sugar maple
North Carolina	Dogwood	Cardinal	(None)
North Dakota	Prairie rose	Western meadow lark	Elm

175

State	Flower	Bird	Tree
Ohio	Scarlet carnation	Cardinal	Ohio buckeye
Oklahoma	Mistletoe	Scissor-tailed flycatcher	Redbud
Oregon	Oregon grape	Western meadow lark	Douglas fir
Pennsylvania	Mountain laurel	Ruffed grouse	Eastern hemlock
Rohde Island	Violet	Rhode Island red	Red maple
South Carolina	Yellow jessamine	Carolina wren	Cabbage palmetto
South Dakota	Pasque flower	Ring-necked pheasant	Black Hills spruce
Tennessee	Iris	Mockingbird	Tulip poplar
Texas	Bluebonnet	Mockingbird	Pecan
Utah	Sego lily	California gull	Blue spruce
Vermont	Red clover	Hermit thrush	Sugar maple
Virginia	American dogwood	Cardinal	American dogwood
Washington	Coast rhododendron	Willow goldfinch	Western hemlock
West Virginia	Rosebay rhododendron	Cardinal	Sugar maple
Wisconsin	Butterfly violet	Robin	Sugar maple
Wyoming	Indian paintbrush	Meadow lark	Cottonwood
District of Columbia	American beauty rose	Woodthrush	Scarlet oak

State Nicknames

"Old North"—North Carolina
"Empire State"—New York
"Palmetto State"—South Carolina
"Little Rhody"—Rhode Island
"Buckeye State"—Ohio
"Nutmeg State"—Connecticut
"Blue Hen"—Delaware
"Granite"—New Hampshire
"Keystone State"—Pennsylvania
"Creole State"—Louisiana

"Sucker State" (Succor)—Illinois
"Hoosier State"—Indiana
"Bay State"—Massachusetts
"Lone Star State"—Texas
"Pine Tree State"—Maine
"Old Dominion"—Virginia

State Songs

Alaska—"Alaska's Flag"
Indiana—"On the Banks of the Wabash"
Hawaii—"Aloha Oe"
Kentucky—"My Old Kentucky Home"
Maryland—"Maryland! My Maryland!"
Missouri—"Missouri Waltz"
Wisconsin—"On Wisconsin"

State Holidays

January 8—Battle of New Orleans. Louisiana.

January 19—Robert E. Lee's Birthday. Alabama, Arkansas, Florida, Georgia, Kentucky, Mississippi, North Carolina, South Carolina, Tennessee, Texas, Virginia.

February 12—Anniversary of Oglethorpe's landing in 1733. Georgia.

March 2—Sam Houston Memorial Day. Texas.

March 25—Maryland Day. Maryland.

April 13—Thomas Jefferson's Birthday. Alabama, Missouri, Virginia.

April 19—Patriots' Day. (Anniversity of the Battle of Lexington, April 19, 1775; also known as "Paul Revere Day." Maine, Massachusetts.

May 20—Anniversity of signing of the Mecklenburg Declaration of Independence. North Carolina.

June 15—Pioneer Day. Idaho.

July 24—Pioneer Day. Utah.

August 16—Anniversity of the Battle of Bennington, August 16, 1777. Vermont.

September 12—Defenders' Day. Maryland.
October 1—Missouri Day. Missouri.

EARLY AMERICAN FORTS

Revolutionary War	*Civil War*
Fort Ticonderoga	Fort Sumter
Fort William Henry	Fort Moultrie
Fort Duquesne	Fort Donelson
	Fort Fisher

Answers to Quotations on Page 167

1. John Dickinson (Pennsylvania)
2. James Otis (Massachusetts)
3. Thomas Paine
4. General Henry Lee
5. Senator Macy (New York)*
6. Franklin D. Roosevelt
7. Napoleon Bonaparte
8. Charles C. Pinckney
9. Andrew Carnegie
10. Thomas Jefferson
11. John Paul Jones
12. Stephen Collins Foster†
13. Washington Irving
14. Andrew Jackson
15. Calvin Coolidge
16. Theodore Roosevelt

* The "spoils system" relates to President Jackson's policy of turning out office-holders and replacing them with members of his own party.
† These words were written on a piece of paper and found in Foster's pocket when he died.

178